BEST OF

Bangkok

China Williams

Best of Bangkok
2nd edition – February 2005
First published – September 2002

Published by Lonely Planet Publications Pty Ltd
ABN 36 005 607 983

Australia Head Office, Locked Bag 1, Footscray, Vic 3011
☎ 03 8379 8000 fax 03 8379 8111
📠 talk2us@lonelyplanet.com.au

USA 150 Linden St, Oakland, CA 94607
☎ 510 893 8555 toll free 800 275 8555
fax 510 893 8572
📠 info@lonelyplanet.com

UK 72–82 Rosebery Avenue, London EC1R 4RW
☎ 020 7841 9000 fax 020 7841 9001
📠 go@lonelyplanet.co.uk

This title was commissioned in Lonely Planet's Melbourne
office and produced by: **Commissioning Editor** Kalya
Ryan **Coordinating Editor** Laura Gibb **Coordinating
Cartographer** Amanda Sierp **Layout Designer** Steven
Cann **Editor** Jocelyn Harewood **Managing Cartographer**
Corinne Waddell **Cover Designer** Julie Rovis **Project
Manager** Andrew Weatherill **Mapping Development**
Paul Piaia **Thanks to** Bruce Evans, Louise McGregor,
Darren O'Connell, Stefanie Di Trocchio, Adriana
Mammarella, Kate McDonald, Quentin Frayne, Ray
Thomson & Jennifer Garrett.

© Lonely Planet Publications Pty Ltd 2005.

All rights reserved.

Photographs by Lonely Planet Images and Richard
I'Anson except for the following: p48 Nicholas Reuss/
Lonely Planet Images; p49 Frank Carter/Lonely Planet
Images; p50 Chris Mellor/Lonely Planet Images; p51
Richard Nebesky/Lonely Planet Images; p82 Juliet Combe/
Lonely Planet Images. **Cover photograph** Traders on their
boats at the floating market – Damnoen Saduak, Chris
Mellor/Lonely Planet Images. All images are copyright of
the photographers unless otherwise indicated. Many of
the images in this guide are available for licensing from
Lonely Planet Images: 📠 www.lonelyplanetimages.com

ISBN 1 74059 765 6

Printed by Markono Print Media Pte Ltd, Singapore.

Lonely Planet and the Lonely Planet logo are trademarks
of Lonely Planet and are registered in the US Patent and
Trademark Office and in other countries.

Lonely Planet does not allow its name or logo to be
appropriated by commercial establishments, such as
retailers, restaurants or hotels. Please let us know of any
misuses: 📠 www.lonelyplanet.com/ip

HOW TO USE THIS BOOK

Colour-Coding & Maps

Each chapter has a colour code along the
banner at the top of the page which is also
used for text and symbols on maps (eg all
venues reviewed in the Highlights chapter
are orange on the maps). The fold-out
maps inside the front and back covers are
numbered from 1 to 7. All sights and venues
in the text have map references; eg (3, B5)
means Map 3, grid reference B5. See p128
for map symbols.

Prices

Multiple prices listed with reviews (eg 70/50B)
usually indicate adult/concession admission to
a venue. Concession prices can include senior,
student, member or coupon discounts. Meal cost
and room rate categories are listed at the start of
the Eating and Sleeping chapters, respectively.

Text Symbols

☎	telephone
✉	address
💻	email/website address
$	admission
🕓	opening hours
ℹ	information
🚆	train
⊖	subway
🚌	bus
🚗	taxi
⚓	ferry/boat
P	parking available
♿	wheelchair access
✗	on site/nearby eatery
☂	child-friendly venue
V	good vegetarian selection

Contents

From the Publisher

AUTHOR

China Williams

For the past two years, China Williams has gone bicoastal, splitting time between the unlikely duo of Bangkok, Thailand, and Portland, Maine. Upon each stateside return, she wishes she could sneak Bangkok's street food vendors and plastic bag drinks and the art of chit-chat through customs. In the reverse direction, she'd take bleach, high-quality sound systems and emissions control.

Thanks to my hubby, Matt Baum, for his tireless investigation of Bangkok's good food and drink. To Nuan and company for the Chinatown tour, Jean Wu and Daniel Cooney for the Mizu trip, Rafael D Frankel and Susan Keppelman for their respective neighbourhood tips, and Mason and Luka, helpful as always. Final nods to the Bangkok Tourist Bureau and the talented Lonely Planet staff.

The 1st edition of this book was written by Rebecca Turner.

PHOTOGRAPHER

Richard I'Anson

Richard I'Anson is a Melbourne-based travel photographer. He travels frequently to both remote and well known destinations photographing people and places for clients and his stock collection.

Richard received his first camera as a gift from his parents when he was 16, and hasn't stopped taking photographs since. After studying photography, film and television at Rusden State College, he worked in a camera store and photographic lab before going freelance in 1982. Since then, his work has been widely published and exhibited around the world.

Lonely Planet has been using Richard's photographs for 15 years and his work has been featured in over 300 editions of LP titles. Lonely Planet has published his two pictorial books, Chasing Rickshaws and Rice Trails: A Journey through the Ricelands of Asia and Australia, both collaborations with Lonely Planet co-founder Tony Wheeler, and his best-selling book Travel Photography: A Guide to Taking Better Pictures, now in its second edition. Richard has also helped to establish Lonely Planet Images, a commercial photo library specialising in travel-related imagery.

SEND US YOUR FEEDBACK

We love to hear from travellers – your comments keep us on our toes and help make our books better. Our well-travelled team reads every word on what you loved or loathed about this book. Although we cannot reply individually to postal submissions, we always guarantee that your feedback goes straight to the appropriate authors, in time for the next edition – and the most useful submissions are rewarded with a free book. To send us your updates – and find out about Lonely Planet events, newsletters and travel news – visit our award-winning website: 🖥 www.lonelyplanet.com/feedback.

Note: We may edit, reproduce and incorporate your comments in Lonely Planet products such as guidebooks, websites and digital products, so let us know if you don't want your comments reproduced or your name acknowledged. For a copy of our privacy policy visit 🖥 www.lonelyplanet.com/privacy.

Introducing Bangkok

Also known as 'The City Where Anything Goes But the Traffic', Bangkok is the modern Asian metropolis at its steamiest and most exhilarating. Part futuristic, part timeless, Bangkok juggles the best (and worst) of both worlds: old temples sit in the shadows of skyscrapers and luxury cars speed past coughing motorised three-wheelers *(túk-túk)*. Well-travelled bilinguals sip wine in stylish cocoons, while taxi drivers leashed with protective amulets gulp down energy drinks at rickety sidewalk stalls. A modern world orbits recklessly around a serene core found in the winding *soi*, where small villages of tight-knit families carry on as if the outside world never visited tiny Siam – the devout still feed the monks on their daily alms route and neighbours shuffle through the day with good food and conversation.

Just like any good Buddhist, you have to struggle to reach enlightenment in Bangkok, but when it hits you'll understand that famous Thai smile. En route to appreciating this boiling pot of contradictions, you'll be thwarted by heat, noise and traffic. Those frustrating moments are just therapeutic massage; the city is kneading you into its fluid mind-set. Cast aside your cultural rigidity and join the collective cult of having fun (or *sànùk,* as the locals say) – graze through the day at the ubiquitous street stalls, let your money flow freely at the energetic shopping malls or claustrophobic markets, or watch the passing circus on ever-carousing Th Khao San.

Between Sathon Neua and Sathon Tai, Bangkok's traditional artery, the canal

Neighbourhoods

Half the fun of 'seeing' Bangkok is getting there – no small task when the city is a multi-tentacled beast that confounds any presumptuous map.

Bangkok sprawls as impetuously as its most prominent landmark, Mae Nam Chao Phraya (Chao Phraya River). The more predictable railway line heading north from Hualamphong train station neatly divides the central city area into old and new Bangkok.

Old Bangkok cradles **Ko Ratanakosin**, the original royal district of religious monuments. Following the river north is charming **Banglamphu**, a residential neighbourhood of yellow and green shophouses and the famous backpacker spectacle of Th Khao San. Sitting astride Banglamphu like a veteran mahout is **Dusit**, home to Vimanmek Teak Mansion and the current royal residence, Chitlada Palace.

Swarming either side of Hualamphong to the river is bustling **Chinatown**. **Phahurat** (Little India) occupies the outer west. Near the Oriental Hotel (p36) you'll find the former European mercantile district, sprinkled with crumbling colonial-style buildings and grand churches (p30) more at home in piazzas than in circuitous *soi*.

The newer Bangkok is centred around Silom, Sukhumvit and Siam Square, which are crowded with skyscrapers, traffic and neon lights. **Th Silom** is a clogged artery that connects the river to the southern boundary of Lumphini Park and boasts infamous Patpong. Th Withayu is one of many wards for foreign embassies.

Credit-card addicts, as well as fashion-obsessed teenagers, leapfrog between shopping centres in

Standing there in a stupa

the **Siam Square** area bordering Th Phra Ram I. Thanks to the Skytrain and elevated walkways, shoppers enjoy near-continuous climate control.

Following Th Phra Ram I eastward leads to Th Sukhumvit's marathon run to the Gulf of Thailand. This is the executive-expat address, where satellite communities of Italians, Japanese, Germans and others ease homesickness with regular visits to restaurants specialising in their respective national dishes. Th Sukhumvit, Sois 3 and 5, is known as Little Arabia.

Off the Beaten Track

Noise, crowds, language barriers. To get away from it all:

- take a longtail boat down through the Thonburi canals (p52)
- join a meditation class at Wat Mahathat (p41)
- pretend you're an ancient Thai princess at Lettuce Farm Palace (p21)
- have all your cares kneaded and pummelled away during a traditional massage (p42)

Itineraries

Bangkok's heat, humidity and confusing layout can wilt the hardiest sightseer. Be flexible with your expectations and leave lots of room for wandering – where you'll stumble upon the weird and the wacky (footpath facials, dead-end streets claimed as chicken yards, and motorcycles overloaded with crates of eggs).

> **Worst of Bangkok**
> - traffic gridlock and pollution
> - oppressive heat and humidity
> - 'Hello! Where you go?' from dodgy taxi-drivers and touts

DAY ONE

Head across to the Grand Palace, Wat Phra Kaew (pp8-9), Wat Pho (p10) and Amulet Market (p55). Catch a river express boat to Banglamphu for lunch at Ton Pho (p69). Souvenir-shop at Th Khao San Market (p55) and stick around for the nightly parade.

DAY TWO

Catch the river express boat to Chinatown (p15) and wander till you drop. Recuperate in air-conditioned MBK shopping centre (p54), then dip into Thai architecture at Jim Thompson's House (p19). Grab a sunset drink at Vertigo (p86), pop over for dinner at Eat Me Restaurant (p77) and polish off the night at a Patpong go-go bar (p87) or Soi 4 dance clubs.

DAY THREE

If it is a weekend, catch the Skytrain to Chatuchak (p20). Explore Dusit Park (pp16-17) or climb the Golden Mount at Wat Saket (p18). Join the crowd at a *muay thai* (Thai boxing) match (p93) or eat at Vientiane Kitchen (p74). Bid farewell to the City of Angels at Brown Sugar (p89).

Bangkok has road rules, despite appearances to the contrary

Highlights

GRAND PALACE & WAT PHRA KAEW (3, B5)

The Grand Palace and Wat Phra Kaew (Temple of the Emerald Buddha) are two of the holiest sites in all of Thailand. These pilgrimage destinations are also Bangkok's finest tourist destinations because of the artistically superb architecture.

Wat Phra Kaew's riotous display of colours and forms – bell-shaped *chedi*, winged eaves connecting rib-cages of terracotta roofs and statues of guardian spirits attired in porcelain mosaics – easily distract first-time visitors from paying homage to the namesake figure. Housed in the main hall amid lavish ornamentation, the diminutive Emerald Buddha occupies a much greater role in Thailand's religious and national identity than its size suggests; it measures only 66cm and is actually carved of nephrite, a type of jade. The figure was discovered in northern Thailand in the 15th century when a *chedi* was split open by lightning. While being transported to a new location, the figure supposedly lost its plaster covering in a fall, revealing its splendid green appearance. Laotian invaders reportedly stole the sacred Buddha from Chiang Mai in the mid-16th century, but it was retrieved in battle by General Taksin, thus bestowing divine approval on the new reign.

An ancient ceremony acknowledging the figure's royal position requires the king to change the Emerald Buddha's robes every season (hot, rainy and cool). An old set of costumes is on display in the temple museum.

In the quieter and shadier corners of the complex are arcades lined with Rama I–era murals that tell the entire *Ramakian* story. To see the story from start to finish, work your way around clockwise from the northern gate.

Wat Phra Kaew is located next to the Grand Palace on vast grounds consecrated when Rama I moved the capital to Bangkok in

Trees trimmed by the royal poodle-barber

1782. Successive kings and their families lived in the palace compound until Rama V (King Chulalongkorn) moved the royal seat to Dusit (pp16-7). Previous kings housed their substantial harems in Chakri Mahaprasat (Grand Palace Hall), built in 1882 by a British architect, who instilled it with features reminiscent of the Renaissance and Ratanakosin (old Bangkok) style. Amarindra Hall, a former hall of justice, is now used for coronations.

A strict dress code is enforced here; you should wear closed-toed shoes, long pants or skirts, and shirts with sleeves. If you don't pass the dress inspection, you can borrow proper attire from the main office. Remove your shoes before entering the main chapel of Wat Phra Kaew. Buy tickets inside the complex and ignore any touts outside the gates who say the temple is closed or recommend other minor temples to visit; these are all preludes to the infamous gem scam.

Ramakian

The story of *Ramakian*, the Thai version of the epic Indian *Ramayana*, starts with Rama and his bride Sita, whose hand he won in a competition to string a magic bow. The young couple are banished to the forest along with Rama's brother, Lak, where the evil king Ravana disguises himself as a hermit in order to kidnap Sita. He distracts her protectors by creating a beautiful deer for the men to hunt. Rama joins forces with Hanuman, the monkey king, to attack Ravana and rescue Sita. Great diversions occur en route to the final fairytale ending including a Sita-impersonator faking her death, the great clash of opposing armies and the killing of Ravana by Rama's magic bow and arrow. After withstanding a loyalty test of fire, Sita and Rama are triumphantly reunited.

An army of monkeys can come in handy; scene from *Ramakian*, Wat Phra Kaew

WAT PHO (3, B5)

You might visit Wat Phra Kaew out of cultural obligation, but you should visit Wat Pho for pure enjoyment. Rarely crowded, the rambling temple claims a 16th-century birthday, pre-dating the city itself. It is also the country's biggest temple. Still not impressed? How about Wat Pho's primary Buddha – an incredible reclining figure that nearly dwarfs its sizable shelter. Symbolic of Buddha's death and passage into nirvana, the reclining Buddha measures 45m and is gilded with gold leaf. Lining the soles of the feet is a magnificent mother-of-pearl inlay depicting the 108 auspicious *laksana* (traits) that signify the birth of a pre-destined Buddha.

This temple isn't just a one-hit wonder. You can wander uninterrupted past a miniature village of porcelain-tiled *chedi*; the four largest commemorate the first four reigns of the Chakri dynasty. A replica mountain in the approximate centre of the complex is home to playful statues of hermits and giraffes.

In an effort to preserve Thai traditional medicine, Rama III appointed Wat Pho as the national repository for the dying art. Instructional texts and anatomical drawings were inscribed on stone slabs and placed within the complex. An affiliated training school (p42) operates nearby.

INFORMATION

- ☎ 0 2222 5910
- ✉ bounded by Th Chetuphon, Th Maharat, Th Sanamchai & Th Thai Wang
- 💲 20B
- 🕗 8am-5pm
- 🚌 501, 507, 508
- ⛴ Tha Tien or Tha Chang
- ♿ good
- 🍴 Krisa Coffee Shop (p69)

Teaching by example: non-reclining Buddha

The Palm Knows

Tucked into the northern corner of Wat Pho is a bustling fortune-telling pavilion, where palm-readers translate the hands' mysterious lines into general advice for love, health and career success. Typically a palm-reader will want to know the client's day of the week and time of birth (which have a greater significance than the month or date do in Thai astrology).

WAT ARUN (3, B6)

Looking more like a weapon of war, Wat Arun commands as much visual respect as its history would demand. It was here, on the Thonburi side of the river, that Taksin resurrected the Thai capital after the fall of Ayuthaya. What was then a local shrine was transformed by the new ruler into the seat of power, sanctified by the presence of the Emerald Buddha. But, alas, the Temple of Dawn (so named for Taksin's literal and metaphoric arrival in 1767) lost its bid for monarchical monogamy with the crowning of a new king and a new royal monument in Bangkok.

The central *praang* (a corn-cob-shaped stupa) rises to a height of 82m and mimics the aggressive architectural style of Angkor Wat. Not visible from a distance, the *praang* is colourfully attired with a mosaic of patterned porcelain, used as ballast in Chinese sailing ships calling at Bangkok's port. Climb the steep stairs to a base-level terrace for a close-up of Buddhist and Hindu imagery. *Kinnari* (half-human–half-bird) hold up the tower's tiered layers, while the terraces are adorned with figures of Buddhas, Indra (Hindu god of the sky) and Erawan (Indra's elephant mount). A pair of *yaksha* (giants) stand sentry to the main chapel, and Phra Pai, the god of wind, is artistically frozen astride his horse nearby.

INFORMATION

- ☎ 0 2891 1149
- ✉ Th Arun Amarin, Thonburi
- 💲 20B
- 🕙 9am-5pm
- 🚢 cross-river ferry from Tha Tien (2B)
- ♿ fair
- 🍴 Krisa Coffee Shop (p69)

Temple Talk

Not quite sure whether it's a *chedi*, *bòt* or *wíhǎan*? A *wíhǎan* is the main prayer hall and holds the temple's Buddha images. A *bòt* is a consecrated hall for monk ordinations. Both are four-sided structures with roof flourishes symbolic of the *naga*, a mythical serpent. *Chedi*, also known as stupa, are typically bell-shaped monuments containing fragments of the Buddha or a king's ashes.

Quite a climb: Wat Arun

MAE NAM CHAO PHRAYA (2, B1-6)

Along mighty Mae Nam Chao Phraya (Chao Phraya River), boxy skyscrapers achieve modern-art sensibilities and traditional houses peek out between warehouses and busy boat docks. As evening sets in, cool river breezes mellow the harsh temperatures and the blinding sun slips into serene streaks of reds and golds.

INFORMATION

- $ 6-15B depending on destination
- boats leave 7am-6.45pm
- Tha Wat Ratchasingkhon to Tha Nonthaburi
- inaccessible
- Rim Fung Restaurant (☎ 0 2525 1742; to the right of the river pier in Nonthaburi)

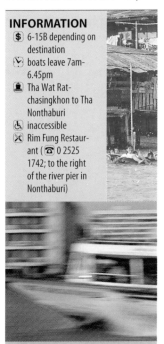

The best way to explore the watery side of Bangkok is aboard a humble river ferry, which loops from Wat Ratchasingkhon (2, A5) north to Nonthaburi (2, A3). At docks along the way, the ferry discharges crowds of map-toting tourists, commuting office clerks and groups of monks. (The back of the starboard-side is reserved for monks; women should opt for the port-side.)

Starting an upriver journey from Sathon (4, A6), you'll notice the old *faràng* (Westerners') quarter on your right, signalled by the **Oriental Hotel** (p36; 4, A5) and crumbling **Old Customs House** (p36; 3, E9). This is where Bangkok's first multinational companies were headquartered; notice how these grand old buildings were designed to receive visitors from the water rather than from the interior street.

Tour-boat-watching from the privacy of home

It's all about the journey: Mae Nam Chao Phraya ferry

Around Tha Ratchawong, the river brushes up against **Chinatown** (p15) and its cubby-holed warehouses that shelter goods before scrappy coolies can haul them (by hand-truck or motorcycle) deeper into the districts' many shops and markets.

After a while, striking **Wat Arun** (p11) looms on your left and then ornate **Grand Palace** and **Wat Phra Kaew** (pp8-9) on your right – forming a triangular convergence of sacred sites and the ancient core of the city.

Not far away is **Khlong Bangkok Noi** (p52), an incision into a community wired by water rather than asphalt. This canal spur was actually the original course of Mae Nam Chao Phraya that was bypassed in the 16th century by the present-day course to ease navigation to Ayuthaya. Glimpses of old Bangkok – with its stilted homes using the river as everything, including the kitchen sink – are best viewed from this serpentine canal reached by hiring a longtail boat (p52). Boat tours often stop at **Wat Suwannaram**, where you'll see exquisite *jataka* murals.

North of the elegant **Saphan Phra Ram VIII** (suspension bridge; 2, C2), concrete dissipates into greenery, stilt houses and sunburned temples. The daily cycle of river life carries on – locals wash and fish as pregnant barges lumber past carrying sand from deposits at the mouth of the river to construction sites further upstream. The final stop is **Nonthaburi**, a busy community known for durian (the spiky-armoured fruit that is so pungent that passengers cannot carry it on commercial buses or airlines). This is also the launching point for trips to secluded **Ko Kret** (p51).

Ghostly Towers

Abandoned construction projects – reminders of the 1997 economic crash – are common features of Bangkok's skyline. But the most haunting orphan is the seemingly operational Sofitel (3, A5). Everything looks to be in order here, until nightfall, when the absence of interior lights betrays the building's abandonment. Some say the building never opened because of faulty construction, others blame bankruptcy – but all agree that it is a hulking, postmodern symbol of bad luck.

CHATUCHAK WEEKEND MARKET (2, B3)

Bangkok's most famous flea market bears the city's quintessential stamp of excess. Imagine super-sizing the average Thai market with its narrow

INFORMATION

- ✉ Th Kamphaeng Phet, Chatuchak Park & Th Phahonyothin
- $ free
- ☉ Sat & Sun 8am-6pm
- ⓘ information centre (☎ 0 2272 4440; near Section 25)
- Ⓜ Mo Chit
- Ⓞ Chatuchak Park
- ♿ limited
- ✕ Viva's (☎ 0 2272 4783; Section 26, btwn Sois 1 & 2)

passageways lined with merchandise, and you've got a close approximation of Chatuchak. Silks, extra-small fashions for Siam Square princesses, fighting cocks and fighting fish, fluffy puppies to fulfil Thai's cute quota and souvenirs for the insatiable *faràng* – if it can be sold in Thailand, then you'll find it here. From basic to clubby, clothes dominate most of the market, where many young designers unveil their wares. Keep an eye out for the second-hand clothes that have obviously emigrated from Western closets.

Your wallet may already be champing at the bit, but go prepared and go early as there are hundreds of thousands of visitors a day, crowding and sweating in the precious open spaces. In theory, Chatuchak is organised into logical, numbered sections but good luck trying to decipher this while pointy elbows nudge you along. Do a little reconnaissance work with Nancy Chandler's *Map of Bangkok*, which is available at English-language bookstores such as Asia Books (p63).

You really can't see it all in one day, even if you have superhuman powers of resisting heat (there's no air-conditioning) and claustrophobia. If dehydration sets in (a sudden feeling of everything sucking), head towards the information centre where there is a concentration of cafés.

Wildlife for Sale

Although the Thai government has launched numerous raids, Chatuchak remains a conduit for illegally traded wildlife. Smuggled out of the rainforests of Indonesia and Malaysia, orang-utans, tigers and other animals prized for their medicinal or culinary merits arrive in the hidden showrooms for export to East Asia.

Go mad stocking up on trinkets, but try to leave the market's fluffy puppies behind

CHINATOWN (3, C6)

Crowded, noisy and oh-so-exhilarating – Chinatown is atomic energy bundled into blazing neon signs, arteries clogged with belching buses, and overflowing footpaths. Each block specialises in selling or making a certain product – rubber bathplugs here, guns and ammo there, and just beyond that, painted signs and coffins.

The main artery, **Th Yaowarat**, lends its name to the district and is crowded with gold shops, sealed glass-front buildings looking a lot like Chinese altars. **Wat Mangkon Kamalawat** (p28) is one of many cultural hybrids, where Chinese and Thai deities enjoy equal veneration. Draining the district towards the southeast, Th Yaowarat collides with **Th Charoen Krung** near the revered **Wat Traimit** (p25).

Beneath its cacophonous façade are hidden universes of winding alleys. **Sampeng Lane** (p57) is now a wholesome market, formerly a red-light district of opium dens, gambling houses and brothels. Claiming mythic longevity is Talat Gao (Old Market) on **Trok Itsaranuphap** (p38). South of Wat Traimit on the riverside of Th Charoen Krung is a network of *soi* (lanes) known as **Talat Noi** (3, E7; btwn Th Songwat & Th Si Phraya), a labyrinth of machine shops.

Since arriving as labourers to help build the new capital, the Chinese in Bangkok have risen to achieve royal appointments and found financial dynasties within a few generations. The present king even claims Chinese heritage, as does half of Bangkok.

INFORMATION

- ✉ bounded by Th Chakraphet, Th Charoen Krung & the river
- 🚌 508, 73, 53
- ⚓ Tha Ratchawong
- ♿ fair
- ✖ Shangarila (p71)

DONT MISS

- funerary shops on Trok Itsaranuphap (p38)
- eating at Pet Tun Jao Tha (p70) or Hong Kong Noodles (p70)
- getting lost
- Chinese New Year & Vegetarian Festival (p84)

East meets East in Bangkok's Chinatown

DUSIT PARK (3, E1)

Leafy and peaceful, Dusit Park is the three-dimensional scrapbook made by Rama V (King Chulalongkorn) of his European tour. Ushering in a new age and a new millennium, Rama V moved the royal residence from the Grand Palace to this European-inspired complex. Reflecting the king's ingenious use of Western influences, **Abhisek Dusit Throne Hall** (built 1904) is a tasteful mélange of Moorish palaces and Victorian mansions that retains a distinctly Thai character. Porticoes topped with terracotta, tiles decorated with elaborate wooden fretwork and stained-glass panels pose in front of a sweeping lawn. Today the hall is used to exhibit an exceptional collection of regional handicrafts. Intricate patterns are inscribed on silverware using metallic-coloured beetles' wings (*málaeng tháp*), blocks of teak are carved into florid detail and the work of silkworms is woven into striking reflections of the regional silk-weaving traditions. Voluptuous bamboo baskets boast dizzying geometric patterns. The pieces are made by members of the Foundation for the Promotion of Supplementary Occupations and Related Techniques (SUPPORT), sponsored by Queen Sirikit, to keep traditional skills alive.

An enormous golden-teak mansion, **Vimanmek Teak Palace**, was selected to house the king and his wife, children and concubines. In 1868 the mansion was originally located on Ko Si Chang, in the Gulf of Thailand, but was dismantled and reassembled, reputedly without nails, on this new palace complex in 1901. The king took a three-storey octagonal apartment for himself and decorated his new home with more than a passing reference to the grand Victorian palaces he had seen in Europe. Women lived in a special green-coloured wing (the only men allowed inside were Rama V, a monk, a doctor and small boys) and a giant mirror on the main staircase was installed as a security device.

Vimanmek Teak Palace's 81 rooms are elegant and overwhelmingly pastel, with walls painted either beige, blue, green, ivory or pink. But the highlight, besides the

INFORMATION

- ☎ 0 2628 6300
- ✉ bounded by Th Ratchawithi, Th U-Thong & Th Ratchasima
- 💲 100/50B (free with Grand Palace ticket)
- 🕙 9.30am-3.15pm
- 🚌 510, 72, 70
- 🚊 Tha Thewet
- ♿ limited
- 🍴 park restaurant

The mansion to which one is accustomed

DON'T MISS

- Vimanmek Palace's TV room and Rama IX's original artwork
- exploring the gardens
- traditional dance performances

architecture, is seeing Rama V's personal effects and antiques – among them, grand pianos, beautiful Ching dynasty pieces and the first menu in Thailand – and getting an insight into how the royals lived. Viewing of the mansion is by guided tour only; tours run every 30 minutes.

Until it was reopened in 1982, the mansion hadn't been used since 1932. A mark in the floorboards is the only reminder of its WWII bombing. Thais believe an important Buddha image protected the building from great damage during the bomb attack.

Wandering the grounds, you'll stumble upon smaller residences formerly inhabited by the monarch's extended family, now hosting various museums. Near the Th Ratchawithi entrance, two residence halls display the **HM King Bumiphol Photography Exhibitions**, collections of photographs and paintings by the present monarch. Among many loving photos of his wife and children are also historic pictures of the king playing the clarinet with Benny Goodman

Brace yourself for the cymbal clash

and Louis Armstrong in 1960. Nearby is the **Ancient Cloth Museum** (p31) and tucked away beside the Th U-Thong exit is the **Royal Elephant Museum** (p32).

Because this is royal property, visitors must dress appropriately (long pants or skirts, and shirts with sleeves); sarongs are available if your lower half isn't covered properly.

Rama V saw European architecture, evoked in Abhisek Dusit Throne Hall, during his travels

WAT SAKET & GOLDEN MOUNT (3, D4)

From the top of Wat Saket's Golden Mount, Bangkok is transformed into a breezy city of terracotta-roofed temples and distant glimpses of modernity. American writer Frank Vincent enjoyed this view in 1871 and recorded in *The Land of the White Elephant* that 'the general appearance of Bangkok is that of a large primitive village, situated in and mostly concealed by a virgin forest of almost impenetrable density'. From the ground it might seem like a quaint depiction, but from this view Bangkok reveals itself as a misunderstood village, now eclipsed by an impenetrable concrete jungle instead of virgin forests. The meditative walk up the steady set of stairs circumnavigates the artificial hill lined with heavy vines and tombstones bearing pictures of the deceased. Near the top, a row of ponderous brass bells are rung by the faithful before they reach the golden *chedi* that caps the top. The annual temple fair is worth a visit for the candlelit procession.

INFORMATION

- ☎ 0 2621 0576
- ✉ Th Chakkaphatdi
- $ 10B
- ◷ 7.30am-5.30pm
- ⊟ 508, 511
- ⛴ *khlong* taxi to Tha Phan Fah
- ♿ limited
- ✕ Thip Samai (p69)

The hill itself was originally intended to form the body of a giant *chedi*, commissioned by Rama III, but it collapsed due to its soft soil base. It was a ruin until Rama IV built a small *chedi* on its crest boasting a 360-degree view.

At the base of the Golden Mount, you'll find demure Wat Saket, which was built during the time of Rama I and serves more of a religious than artistic role.

Challenging Heaven

Until the 1960s, Golden Mount was the tallest point in Bangkok (a title since ceded to a grove of skyscrapers) and still claims that title in the neighbourhood of Banglamphu.

JIM THOMPSON'S HOUSE (4, D1)

If the art and architecture of Jim Thompson's House doesn't grip you, the story of its former owner will. American-born Thompson was an intriguing chap in both life and death – he disappeared without a trace during an afternoon stroll in Malaysia's Cameron Highlands in 1967. His legacy is a revered Thai silk industry, a collection of Southeast Asian art and a serene assembly of traditional Thai homes.

Six teak houses – reputedly built without nails – occupy the site he bought beside Khlong Saen Saep in 1959 (adhering to Thai traditions, he moved in on an astrologically auspicious day). Thompson, who had served in Thailand during WWII, returned after finding New York City a tad quiet. His art collection and personal possessions, including rare Chinese porcelain pieces and Burmese, Cambodian and Thai artefacts, are displayed throughout the site, which is lush and tropical and punctuated by lotus ponds. You can also poke through his library, the only room with glassed-in windows (he weakened in the end and installed air-conditioning).

But undoubtedly Thompson's keen eye for design was best used to revive a Thai cottage industry under the threat of extinction. He sent samples of hand-woven silk (made by nearby villagers) to European fashion houses, creating a demand for it that continues to this day.

INFORMATION

- ☎ 0 2215 0122
- ✉ Soi Kasem San 2, Th Phra Ram I
- $ 100/50B
- ◷ 9am-5pm
- ⓘ compulsory tours (English & French) every 10 min
- 🚇 National Stadium
- 🚌 508, 73
- ⛴ *khlong* taxi to Ratchathewi
- ♿ fair
- ✗ Jim Thompson Café

Accident or Foul Play?

Conspiracies abound on the fate of Bangkok's most famous expat. Some muse that Jim Thompson was snatched by communist spies, while others say he met his maker between the fangs of a man-eating tiger. Much less fascinating, but far more likely, is that he was run over by a Malaysian truck driver.

Be sure to wear your gourd in the gardens

SKYTRAIN (Bangkok Transport Network map)

When the sightseeing becomes tedious, ascend the crooked stairs to the elevated platforms of one of the world's slickest mass-transit systems. An ingenious solution to incurable gridlock, the Skytrain glides way above the ground-level chaos, connecting Siam Square, Sukhumvit, Silom and Mo Chit. The open-air stations are crowded with Japanese-pop aesthetics: blaring advertisements, beeping plastic toys, and a barrage of ringing mobile phones. Meanwhile, from this viewpoint, you can peer into an ant-colony-like construction site or the garden compounds of the city elite.

INFORMATION

- ☎ 0 2617 7300
- 🖳 www.bts.co.th
- ✉ Sukhumvit and Silom lines intersect at Siam (Th Phra Ram I)
- 💲 10-40B; 100B one-day pass, unlimited rides
- ⏱ 6am-midnight
- ♿ fair
- 🍴 MBK Food Hall (p76)

Though its coverage is limited, the Skytrain is a revolution – trips that used to take an hour or more by car now take 15 minutes, transforming the horizontal mobility of the upwardly mobile. (Skytrain is, however, often criticised for being too expensive for the working class who still rely on the beleaguered bus system.)

Before the system proved its mettle, ever-prescient Bangkokians predicted failure for the project that was 13 years in the making, and debates still simmer over the system's overall reduction of traffic. Itching to expand into the residential areas, the Skytrain system has met with continual delays because decision-makers are unable to agree on a route that passes through the holiest section of Bangkok (Ko Ratanakosin) but doesn't violate protective regulations for the area's sacred temples. But you are free to ignore the municipal in-fighting as you cruise home in style.

Going Nowhere Fast

The walkway from National Stadium Skytrain station to Siam Centre gives a refreshing perspective on Bangkok's notorious traffic – idling automobiles stretch beyond the horizon at least six lanes thick, lending anecdotal evidence to the generous estimate that city traffic travels at an average speed of 5km/h to 6km/h.

Rapid transit: you won't see it coming

LETTUCE FARM PALACE (2, B4)

A wander around the peaceful gardens of Lettuce Farm Palace (Wang Suan Phakkat) and inside its traditional buildings can transport you a million miles from central Bangkok. The palace grounds were once a farm of the same name and, later, were the site of the home of Princess Chumbon of Nakhon Sawan, the architect behind the gardens. But now the palace's six houses, connected by wooden walkways and full of art, antiques and artefacts, are permanently open to the public.

The complex's most famous exhibit, the **Lacquer Pavilion**, sits on stilts at the back of the property. Taken from a monastery near Ayuthaya, the tiny building has an exterior lined with wood carvings and an interior decorated with intricate gold-leaf and black-lacquer *jataka* (stories of the Buddha) and *Ramayana* murals.

INFORMATION

☎ 0 2245 4934
✉ Th Sri Ayuthaya, near Th Rat-chaprarop
$ 100B
🕐 9am-4pm
ℹ information centre below House IV
🚇 Phayathai
🚌 504, 63, 72
♿ fair
✕ Foodloft (p75)

You'll uncover a mixture of stuff in the rest of the buildings. If you're interested in *khon* (classical Thai masked dance) performance, then make sure you head for the small museum just near House VI which shows how the elaborate masks are created and introduces you to the different characters in the *Ramakian* drama. House II has a curious collection of ceremonial fans, while House I boasts a magnificent U-Thong seated Buddha image. Prehistory buffs will have a field day with the exhibits of House V and VI. The princess appears to have been quite the shell and mineral enthusiast, as you'll see by her collections.

DON'T MISS
- the air-conditioned music room
- meeting the pelican who lives on the grounds
- enjoying the solitude just steps from screaming traffic

Knobbed gongs, also known as nipple gongs, at Lettuce Farm Palace

LUMPHINI PARK (4, F4)

A morning visit to Bangkok's green lung is a must-do. Try to get there around 7am, when all the action starts. The pathways are crammed with people gliding into t'ai chi poses or kicking up their heels at aerobics classes. Groups of the elderly settle under trees for what looks like an open-air karaoke session (the warbled songs are most definitely an acquired taste). Beefcakes colonise the weights corner with an air of intimidation. The vendors carefully arrange their stalls of snake blood and bile, popular health tonics. Chess players settle in for a duel to the death, while joggers pound their way around the park. And then it all stops, suddenly, when the royal anthem is played at 8am.

INFORMATION

- ✉ Th Phra Ram IV, btwn Th Withayu & Th Ratchadamri
- 💲 free
- 🕐 5am-8pm
- 🚇 Sala Daeng
- 🅾 Lumphini
- 🚌 504, 505, 507
- ♿ excellent
- 🍴 food stalls on southern boundary

Lumphini Park is named after Buddha's birthplace in Nepal and provides the best free entertainment in town – even more so during the concert performances in the cool months or in kite-flying season, when there are dashing antics in the skies above. For a nominal charge, you can hire one of the paddleboats that putter around the enormous ornamental lake. But you don't need to part with any money in order to experience the feeling that you've escaped from the big smoke, if only for a moment.

And For the Children

Footpaths for energetic sprinters, turtles to feed and a spiffy playground to explore – Lumphini can be appreciated by all ages, especially the pint-sized. Mornings and evenings are good times to hit the park with the little ones and to meet other families enjoying the cool hours of the day.

Excellent spot for a nap

NATIONAL MUSEUM (6, A3)

If the National Museum were a person, it would be a scatterbrained yet brilliant university lecturer. Why? Its collections are top-rate but haphazardly arranged, lacking the censuring measures most museums employ to attract and keep neophytes' attention. A new history wing, complete with computer terminals and audio explanations, gives an uncharacteristically formal chronological tour through Thai history and may be a sign that the arts and artefacts buildings will soon receive a similar makeover.

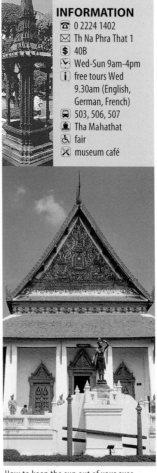

INFORMATION
- ☎ 0 2224 1402
- ✉ Th Na Phra That 1
- 💲 40B
- 🕐 Wed-Sun 9am-4pm
- ℹ free tours Wed 9.30am (English, German, French)
- 🚌 503, 506, 507
- ⚓ Tha Mahathat
- ♿ fair
- 🍴 museum café

Occupying an 18th-century palace, the National Museum – said to be Southeast Asia's biggest – and its exhaustive collections are thematically grouped in different buildings. A handy navigational guide is issued at the ticket booth, but a guided tour may be a better introduction to the important religious art collection.

For the look-and-nod types, pay a visit to the elaborate funeral chariots that have carried the ashes of royalty. You can get insights into the benefits of migration from Room 15, which displays the musical instruments of a Phat Mon ensemble, a popular performance style introduced by the Mon people (whose descendants live on Ko Kret) from Burma. The money collection – including fat Sukhothai coins said to have magical properties and the long *Hoi* money used in the north – is surprisingly fascinating. Before you leave, visit the restored Buddhaisawan (Phutthaisawan) Chapel to see one of Thailand's revered Buddha images, Phra Phuttha Sihing, and the golden teak Tamnak Daeng house nearby.

How to keep the sun out of your eyes

DON'T MISS

- the stone inscription credited to Sukhothai's King Ramakhamhaeng and believed to have established the Thai alphabet
- the Rama V exhibition
- comparing the different artistic styles used to depict Buddha

ROYAL BARGES NATIONAL MUSEUM (3, A3)

A remnant of Thailand's ancient ties to waterways are the ornate and fantastically coloured barges used by the royal family when they travelled. Dating back to Ayuthaya, a royal outing meant a royal barge procession:

hundreds of men rowing sleek, gold-covered boats accompanied by rhythm-makers and royal chanters. In modern times, the elaborate procession is infrequently staged during the *kathin* ceremony (when robes are offered to monks) or during important anniversaries. In the meantime, the royal barges are permanently on display at this museum in Thonburi.

The most revered barge is the swan-shaped boat *Supphannahong* (Golden Swan), an enormous vessel which carries the king, a rowing crew of 50 people, seven umbrella bearers, two helmsmen, two navigators, a flagman, a rhythm-keeper and a chanter. *Supphannahong* is 50m long and made out of a single piece of timber, making it the world's largest dugout boat.

The bow of the *Anantanakarat* is carved to resemble a mythical seven-headed *naga* and is the vessel in which monastic robes are carried. The newest craft to join the fleet is *Narai Song Suban,* which was built to commemorate the king's 50th anniversary.

It's a good idea to take the Chao Phraya shuttle boat or a hired longtail to the museum. Note that if you walk in via the interior curving walkway, you might be hassled by touts.

Take a Bow

The dramatic figureheads protruding from the bows of royal barges are usually based on creatures of Hindu mythology, such as the *garuda* (eagle-man used as as Vishnu's mount), *naga* (multi-headed sea serpent considered guardian of Thai people) and swan (symbol of grace).

The *naga* is a beast you'd want on your side

WAT TRAIMIT (3, E7)

You only visit Wat Traimit (Temple of the Golden Buddha) for one reason – one very big reason: the world's largest golden Buddha image which weighs a whopping 5.5 tonnes and stands 3m tall.

If it wasn't for an opportune accident, this Sukhothai-era image could still be hidden beneath a layer of plaster coating. It wasn't until 1955, when workers began to move the hulking figure out of temporary storage to its long-term home in the current temple, that it fell from the crane, cracking the coating. Rain continued to erode the plaster, which revealed the bewitching golden gleam beneath. Apparently it was a common practice to conceal the most valuable Buddha images under a disguise of plaster during the late Sukhothai and early Ayuthaya periods, when the threat of Burmese invaders was very real (indeed, the invaders eventually brought down the Ayuthaya era). During the chaos that ensued after the fall of Ayuthaya, the true identities of many Buddhas were lost and those that have since revealed themselves are revered and endowed with great religious importance. Now, almost 50 years down the track, the Golden Buddha is beautifully polished and is housed in a modest pavilion in Wat Traimit.

INFORMATION

- ☎ 0 2623 1226
- ✉ Th Traimit
- 💲 20B
- ⏰ 8am–5pm
- 🚌 53
- Ⓜ Hualamphong
- ♿ limited
- 🍴 Hong Kong Noodles (p70)

Visitors enjoy a golden moment

Beautifying Buddha

Thailand's great artistic awakening is often credited to an era spanning the mid-13th to late-14th centuries, during the heyday of northern Thailand's Sukhothai kingdom. Here artisans incorporated techniques from the dominant Khmer and Indian sculptures and developed unique sculptural characteristics. Sukhothai-era Buddhas typically have rounded hair curls and elongated earlobes, creating a graceful and slender effect.

WAT MAHATHAT (3, B4)

The rambling Wat Mahathat compound in Ratanakosin is the most important centre of Buddhist learning in Southeast Asia. The Buddhist university on the site, **Mahathat Rajavidyalaya**, attracts monks from Laos, Cambodia and Vietnam, and is the national centre of the Mahanikai monastic sect.

INFORMATION

- ☎ 0 2221 5999
- ✉ 3 Th Maharat
- 💲 donations accepted
- 🕙 9am-5pm
- 🚌 506, 512, 53
- ⚓ Tha Maharat or Tha Chang
- ♿ fair
- 🍴 Krisa Coffee Shop (p69)

Detail of Wat Mahathat

The Mahanikai sect is one of the two sects that make up the Sangha, or Buddhist brotherhood, in Thailand. Members of both sects adhere to the 227 compulsory monastic vows laid out in the Buddhist scriptures, but there are subtle differences as to how strictly these vows are applied to daily monastic life. For example, Mahanikai monks are permitted to eat twice before noon and are also allowed to accept side dishes, while Thammayut monks must be more disciplined by eating only once a day, before noon, and eating only the food they have contained in their alms bowls.

Wat Mahathat was built in the Ayuthaya period, but it has changed its appearance (through renovation) and its name many times. Over the years, it has evolved into an informal community centre and it is always bustling with the activities of visitors and monks. Lots of curious foreigners wander onto the grounds looking for the daily meditation courses (p41) and the resident English-speaking monks make enthusiastic guides.

Located nearby, outside the temple gates on Th Maharat, is a daily market (*talàat phra khrêuang*; p55) selling Thai herbal medicine remedies and auspicious amulets.

Mahathat Medicine

Traditional Thai medicine combines the traditions of Ayurvedic and Chinese medicine, relying primarily on the power of herbs and of touch (massage). Family-run medicine shops, centred around Wat Mahathat, sell herbs that are used to treat various ailments, from high blood pressure to the catch-all condition of 'shock'.

Sights & Activities

TEMPLES & SHRINES

A wat is a Buddhist temple compound, where monks are ordained and lay people make merit. The art, architecture and ritual are major draws for non-Buddhists, but visitors should dress respectfully (closed-toed shoes and covered arms and legs); women shouldn't touch monks or their belongings or pass anything directly to a monk. Remove shoes within temple buildings.

City Pillar (3, B4) Inside this shrine, at the southeastern corner of Sanam Luang is a wooden pillar known as Lak Meuang, representing the founding of the new capital on the eastern side of the river. Worshippers come and make offerings – often by commissioning traditional dances or occasionally with severed pigs' heads and incense – to the spirit of the pillar, which is considered to be the city's guardian. ⊠ cnr Th Ratchadamnoen Nai & Th Lak Meuang $ free ⏱ 8.30am-5.30pm 🚌 506, 507 ⛴ Tha Chang ♿ good

Erawan Shrine (4, F2) This Brahman shrine is engulfed by a perpetual stream of merit-makers and is thick with the haze of incense smoke, overburdened stalls with garlands and caged birds (releasing them earns merit) and the clanging of traditional musicians. Similarly chaotic circumstances surround its beginnings – it was built to ward off bad luck after mishaps delayed construction of the first Erawan Hotel nearby. ☎ 0 2252 8754 ⊠ cnr Th Ploenchit & Th Ratchadamri $ free ⏱ 8am-7pm 🚉 Chitlom 🚌 501, 508, 511, 513 ⛴ khlong taxi to Tha Pratunam ♿ good

Mae Thorani (3, B4) Originally attached to a drinking well, this statue of a female figure wringing out her hair depicts the Buddhist story of Mae Thorani, the earth goddess. Buddha called upon her to help him withstand the temptations of Mara, the force of evil. Mae Thorani obliged by releasing an ocean of water (stored in her hair) and drowning the temptations. ⊠ northern end of Sanam Luang, Th Ratchadamnoen Nai $ free ⏱ 6am-8pm 🚌 507, 53 ♿ good

Sri Gurusingh Sabha Temple (3, D6) This sleek and modern Sikh temple (it's kitted out with elevators and marble throughout) is devoted to Guru Granth Sahib,

That topiarist from the Grand Palace has been to City Pillar, too

one of the last 10 gurus or teachers. You'll find it down a little alleyway off Th Chakraphet.
✉ cnr Th Chakraphet & Th Phahurat $ donations accepted ⏲ 9am-5pm 🚌 53, 73 🚢 Tha Saphan Phut ⛾ good

Sri Mariamman Temple (4, C5) Sri Mariamman Hindu temple is a colourful place of worship in every sense of the word, from the multi-hued main temple built by Tamil immigrants in the 1860s to the eclectic range of people of many faiths and nationalities who come to make offerings. Thais call it Wat Phra Si Kaha Umathewi.
☎ 0 2238 4007
✉ cnr Th Pan & Th Silom $ donations accepted ⏲ 6am-8pm 🚌 502, 504, 505, 15 ⛾ good

Wat Benchamabophit (3, E2) Buddha image buffs find Wat Benchamabophit fascinating. Known as the 'Marble Temple' (it's made of white Carrara marble), it has a collection of 53 Buddha images in different figures and styles. It was built during Rama V's reign (the temple's central Buddha image contains his ashes) and its cruciform

bòt is a pure example of contemporary wat architecture.
✉ cnr Th Sri Ayutthaya & Th Phra Ram V $ 20B ⏲ 8am-5.30pm 🚌 503 ⛾ good

Wat Bowonniwet (6, D2) Monks from around the world come to study at Wat Bowonniwet, home to the Buddhist Mahamakut University, the national headquarters of the Thammayut monastic sect. It may be in the midst of ultra-casual Banglamphu but Bowonniwet is a royal wat (the present king was ordained here) and visitors must be dressed appropriately.
✉ cnr Th Phra Sumen & Th Tanao $ donations accepted ⏲ 8am-5.30pm 🚌 15, 53 🚢 Tha Phra Athit (Banglamphu) ⛾ good

Wat Chong Nonsi (2, B5) In an industrial area south of the city centre, Wat Chong Nonsi is an important Ayuthaya-era temple. Its noted *jataka* murals were painted between 1657 and 1707, and, like the temple itself, haven't ever been renovated – making them pure examples of Ayuthaya styles.
✉ Th Nonsi, off Th Phra Ram III $ donations

accepted ⏲ 8.30am-6pm 🚌 taxi ⛾ fair

Wat Intharawihan (3, D2) This temple at the northern edges of Banglamphu is known for its 32m standing Buddha image in the modern style. Also have a look at the hollow, air-conditioned stupa with a lifelike image of Luang Phaw Toh.
✉ Th Wisut Kasat, near Th Samsen $ donations accepted ⏲ 9am-6pm 🚌 506, 30, 53 ⛾ fair

Wat Mangkon Kamalawat (3, E6) Wat Mangkon Kamalawat has a phenomenal energy and its marble floors with lily pad motif must be trampled by hundreds of people daily. Explore its labyrinthine passageways and you'll find endless shrines, surrounded by visiting devotees of Buddhism, Taoism and Confucianism.
✉ Th Charoen Krung, east of Th Ratchawong $ donations accepted ⏲ 9am-6pm 🚌 501, 507, 73 🚢 Tha Ratchawong ⛾ good

Wat Ratchabophit (3, C5) Commissioned by Rama V soon after he came to the throne, this beautiful temple is decorated with

---

Bangkok for Free
You'll soon discover that almost everything in the City of Angels has a price, but some of the most memorable experiences don't cost a measly satang.
- watching weekend break-dancers in Siam Square (4, D2)
- enjoying evening aerobics at Lumphini (4, F4) or Santichaiprakan Park (6, B1)
- waking up at dawn to find the barefoot, saffron-robed monks on their daily alms route; best seen in Banglamphu (6)
- catching a commissioned dance at City Pillar (3, B4) or Erawan Shrine (4, F2)

Temple Know-how

Punctuating the muddy sky with flamboyant colours and triumphant angles, Thailand's temples are filled with elaborate art acting as visual sermons. Temple murals typically depict an event in the life of Buddha (such as Buddha in the lotus position with his right hand pointed to the ground, shown subduing evil forces), the *jataka* (Buddha's previous lives of hidden princely identities), or heroic battle scenes from *Ramakian*. In the corners of these busy stages, elements of everyday life are depicted – housewives fetching water and fisherman mending nets. A series of lightweight books by the Fine Arts Department, sold at Rim Khob Fah Bookstore (p64), explores temple art and reduces temple fatigue.

Chinese porcelain. European influences are reasonably strong, too – look at the uniforms of the carved guards on the door.
✉ Th Ratchabophit, near cnr of Th Atsadang
💲 donations accepted
🕐 9am-6pm 🚌 60
🛥 Tha Tien ♿ good

One of Wat Benchamabophit's 53 Buddha images

Wat Ratchanatda (3, D4)
This temple was built for Rama III's granddaughter, but these days it's better known for its vibrant amulet market and its metallic castle-like monastery, with many passageways and meditation cells at each intersection.
☎ 0 2224 8807 ✉ cnr Th Ratchadamnoen Klang & Th Mahachai
💲 donations accepted
🕐 9am-5pm 🚌 505, 56 🛥 *khlong* taxi to Tha Phan Fah ♿ fair

Wat Suthat & Giant Swing (3, C5) Wat Suthat holds the highest royal temple grade. Inside the high-ceilinged *wíhăan* are intricate *jataka* murals and Thailand's biggest surviving Sukhothai-era bronze. Just over the road is the Giant Swing (Sao Ching-Cha), the site of a former Brahman festival in honour of Shiva.
☎ 0 2224 9845 ✉ Th Bamrung Meuang 💲 20B
🕐 8.30am-9pm 🚌 508
🛥 *khlong* taxi to Tha Phan Fah ♿ fair

Wat Suwannaram (2, A4)
Located along Khlong Bangkok Noi, Wat Suwan-

naram is an Ayuthaya-era temple, boasting *jataka* murals created by two pre-eminent artists of the Rama III era and considered to be the best remaining temple paintings in the city. But the temple has a dark past – Burmese prisoners-of-war were executed here during King Taksin's era and it was also the location of Bangkok's first concrete crematorium.
✉ Khlong Bangkok Noi, east of Th Charoen Sanit Wong 💲 donations accepted 🕐 9am-6pm
🛥 longtail boat ♿ fair

Wat Thammamongkhon (2, C6) It's a hike out to the outer reaches of Th Sukhumvit, but the sight of the 95m-high *chedi* at Wat Thammamongkhon is pretty incredible. So, too, is the 14-tonne jade sculpture of the Chinese goddess Guanyin. The *chedi*, complete with elevator, comes from a monk's vision of a jade boulder.
☎ 0 2332 8226
✉ 132 Soi 101, Th Sukhumvit 💲 donations accepted 🕐 9am-6pm
🚇 On Nut, then taxi
♿ fair

CHURCHES

Though few in number, Bangkok has some interesting Catholic churches dating back as far as the 17th century. You'll usually find them in the old *faràng* areas – around the Oriental Hotel on the Bangkok side, and the former Portuguese quarter in Thonburi.

No, not Notre-Dame; Assumption Cathedral on Soi Oriental

Assumption Cathedral

(4, A5) This shady church has stunning stained-glass windows and a marble altar. It's in a quiet complex just off Soi Oriental and fronts onto a Bangkok rarity, a small square.
- ☎ 0 2234 8556 ✉ Soi 40, Th Charoen Krung
- $ donations accepted
- 🚉 Saphan Taksin
- 🚌 75, 115, 116 ⛴ Tha Oriental or hotel shuttle boat from Tha Sathon
- ♿ good

Church of the Immaculate Conception (2, A4)

This Catholic church was built by the Portuguese in the 17th century and later taken over by Cambodians fleeing civil war. The current building, overlooking the river, is an 1837 reconstruction of the original church, which is now a museum of holy relics.
- ☎ 0 2243 2617
- ✉ 167 Soi 11, Th Samsen
- $ donations accepted
- ⛴ Tha Thewet ♿ good

Church of Santa Cruz

(3, B7) The Church of Santa Cruz is in the thick of what was the old Portuguese quarter. The current Italianate building was built in 1913 and is popularly known as Wat Kuti Jiin.
- ☎ 0 2466 0347
- ✉ Soi Kuti Jiin, Thonburi
- $ donations accepted
- 🕐 5.30-8.30am, 6-8pm
- ⛴ cross-river ferry from Tha Pak Talad (Atsadang)
- ♿ good

Holy Rosary Church

(3, E8) Vietnamese and Cambodian Catholics rebuilt this Portuguese church more than a century ago – you will be able to see the French inscriptions beneath the Stations of the Cross. During Easter celebrations, an old statue of Christ is carried through the streets.
- ☎ 0 2266 4849
- ✉ 1318 Th Yotha, near River City $ donations accepted 🕐 mass Mon-Sat 6am, Sun 6.15, 8 & 10am ⛴ Tha Si Phraya
- ♿ good

The Portuguese in Bangkok

Of all the European nations that sailed in and out of Thailand's ports, the Portuguese were the first arrivals (thanks to their nearby colony of Malacca in Malaysia) and curried the greatest favour after the fall of the then capital Ayuthaya. Instead of packing up and going home, the Portuguese helped General Taksin secure his new capital and were rewarded with prime real-estate along Mae Nam Chao Phraya. A few grand Catholic churches, now catering to non-European residents, are the Portuguese's surviving legacy.

MUSEUMS

Ancient Cloth Museum

(3, E1) If you're interested in fashion, you should enjoy a poke around this museum, with its well-annotated collection of royal cloth and royals wearing cloth (Queen Sirikit looks a bit groovy in the old B/W photos).

☎ 0 2281 4715 ✉ Dusit Park, Th Ratchawithi $ 100/50B (free with Grand Palace ticket) ⏲ 9.30am-4pm 🚌 510, 72, 70 ♿ good

Ban Kamthieng (5, B2)

Recently renovated, Ban Kamthieng is an excellent merging of traditional architecture with museum-style facts. Exemplifying the Lanna style, this 1844 house shows how a northern Thai commoner lived, with well-signed household tools, video installations on spiritual beliefs and descriptions of family rituals.

☎ 0 2661 6470 ✉ Siam Society, 131 Soi 21 (Soi Asoke), Th Sukhumvit $ 100/50B ⏲ Mon-Sat 9am-5pm 🚇 Asoke ♿ fair

Bangkok Doll Factory & Museum (2, B4)

New and antique dolls dressed in national costumes are displayed for appreciation, while the gift shop sells on-site factory-made dolls, a unique industry that helped preserve, in miniature form, Thai traditional costumes. The museum is difficult to find; the best approach is from Th Sri Ayutthaya heading east. Once you reach the expressway overpass, you'll see a post office on the opposite side of the intersection with Th Ratchaprarop. Follow the soi to the right of the post office and keep an eye out for signs pointing the way to the museum.

☎ 0 2245 3008 ✉ 85 Soi Ratchataphan, Th Ratchaprarop $ free ⏲ Mon-Sat 8am-5pm 🚕 taxi ♿ good

Monk's Bowl Village

(3, D5) The only surviving village of three founded by Rama I, Baan Baht still hand-hammers eight pieces of steel (representing Buddha's eightfold path) into the distinctive alms bowls used by monks to receive morning food donations. Tourists instead of temples are the primary patrons these days and a bowl purchase is usually rewarded with a demonstration.

☎ 0 2223 7970 ✉ Soi Baan Baht, Th Bamrung Meuang $ 600B for a bowl ⏲ 10am-8pm 🚌 508 🚤 *khlong* taxi to Tha Pan Fah ♿ good

National Gallery (6, B3)

This gallery should be so much better than it is. Based in the old mint building, it has collections of traditional and contemporary art that no one seems to care about (you have to turn on the lights yourself). Special exhibits tend to get more attention, and pieces by Rama VI and Rama IX appeal to royalists.

☎ 0 2282 2639 ✉ 4 Th Chao Fa $ 30B

Pieces of eight: alms bowls hand-hammered from eight pieces of steel at Monk's Bowl Village

⏱ Wed-Sun 9am-4pm
🚇 Tha Phra Athit
(Banglamphu) ♿ good

Prasart Museum This museum isn't in Bangkok but we've included it because Prasart Vongsakul's collection of traditional buildings and antiques is a must for any die-hard art and architecture fan. It's tricky to get to so call ahead for directions and let them know you're coming.
☎ 0 2379 3601 ✉ 9 Soi Krungthepkretha 4a, Th Krung Thepkretha, Bang Kapi 💲 500B ⏱ weekends by appointment only 🚌 93 ♿ fair

Royal Thai Elephant Museum (3, E1) Thais consider albinism auspicious, so all white elephants are regarded as royal property (Rama IX keeps one at his palace). Dusit had two stables for keeping white elephants, though today they house this museum, which has displays explaining the ranks of elephants and their important role in Thai society. It's certainly no white elephant.
☎ 0 2628 6300 ✉ Dusit Park, Th Ratchawithi 💲 100/50B (free with Grand Palace ticket) ⏱ 9.30am-4pm 🚌 510, 72, 70 ♿ good

Royal Thai Air Force Museum (2, C2) This museum is strictly for the aficionado who will relish spending a day out around Don Muang. The museum, near wing 6 at the airport, is truly world class, incorporating rare historic planes, including some WWII fighter craft.
☎ 0 2534 1853 ✉ Th Phahonyothin, Don Muang 💲 free ⏱ 8am-4.30pm 🚂 train from Hualamphong to Don Meuang 🚌 503, 520 ♿ limited

Thailand Cultural Centre (2, C4) This top-class, multipurpose arts venue often has temporary art exhibitions, as well as music and drama shows. Check its website for updates.
☎ 0 2247 0028 💻 www.thaicultural center.com ✉ Th Ratchadaphisek (btwn Soi Tiam Ruammit & Th Din Daeng) Ⓜ Thailand Cultural Centre ♿ good

Feeding the Spirits

To the Thais, making merit helps ensure a peaceful life now and in future lives. Merit-making can also benefit deceased relatives and is why many young men enter the monastery after the passing of a grandparent. Thai Buddhism is highly individualistic and its practice isn't limited to the temples. Notice the spirit house, a miniature temple strategically placed outside homes and businesses; this structure provides a comfortable abode for a site's mischievous guardian spirit. Sacred banyan trees, tied with colourful cloth, are doubly endowed because they shelter tree spirits as well as Buddha during his attainment of enlightenment.

Any sacred site or image receives daily offerings – such as three joss sticks, flower garlands, fruit (oranges or coconuts) or a set of three small bowls (containing rice, sweetmeats and water) – along with requests for good health, a good grade on a test or favourable outcomes to other uncertainties.

ART GALLERIES

With a rich tradition of religious art, modern Thai artists are integrating traditional themes with abstract expression. Pick up a copy of the free monthly *Art Connection* brochure, which lists the latest on galleries and shows. Admission isn't charged at these private galleries.

About Studio/About Cafe (3, E7) You've always wanted to be this much of a bohemian – conversant in hip-hop, abstract art and poetry readings. This Chinatown storefront will lead you by the hand to deep-end modern-art appreciation. Watch for openings and posted exhibits as hours vary.
☎ 0 2623 1742-3
✉ 42-46 Th Maitrichit
☽ Mon-Sat noon-9pm
Ⓔ Hualamphong
🚌 53 ♿ good

Gallery F-Stop (5, C2) In an effort to rescue art from the 'dead zones' (traditional museums), many Bangkok restaurants added the works of young talent to the dinner menu. Gallery F-Stop (hosted by Tamarind Café, p74) stands apart as the city's only restaurant-gallery for photography,

and it displays artwork that can be approached without peering over a fellow diner's shoulder.
☎ 0 2663 7421
✉ 27 Soi 20, Th Sukhumvit ☽ 11am-11pm
🚇 Asoke ♿ fair

H Gallery (4, D6) H is a conduit for aspiring abstract artists deemed worthy enough to percolate into New York's top-end galleries. Before jettisoning off to the Big Apple, most shows grace the walls of this neo-colonial gallery or Eat Me restaurant (p77).
☎ 0 1310 4428 ✉ sub-soi off Soi 12, Th Sathon, beside Bangkok Bible College ☽ Wed-Sat noon-6pm 🚇 Chong Nonsi 🚌 17, 22 ♿ fair

Jamjuree Art Gallery (4, D2) Modern spiritual themes and brilliantly-

coloured abstracts from the imaginations of student-artists are displayed in this two-storey contemporary-art space.
☎ 0 2218 3645 ✉ Th Phayathai, Chulalongkorn University, Jamjuree Bldg ☽ 10am-7pm Mon-Fri, noon-4pm Sat & Sun
🚇 Siam 🚌 501, 502 ♿ fair

Kraichitti Gallery (6, C3) Hoping to create an intersection of art and entertainment, this gallery exhibits award-winning photographs of Southeast Asia in an elegant 100-year-old home. The punch line is that all this style and culture is slap bang on grubby Th Khao San.
☎ 0 1623 8284 ✉ Sunset Street Complex, Th Khao San ☽ 3-11pm
🚌 511, 53 ⚓ Tha Phra Athit (Banglamphu)

Bohemian art happens right here in Chinatown

Art for the Other Side

As you walk down Trok Itsaranuphap (3, D7) in Chinatown, keep one eye open for the funerary art shops, crammed with designer shirts, 'passports to heaven' and even houses and paper cars to take loved ones into the next life in style and comfort.

Rotunda Gallery (4, C5)

This gallery in the Neilson-Hays Library sometimes scores good temporary exhibitions. It's a small space but it attracts a varied bunch of artists, from photographers to pen-and-ink types.
☎ 0 2233 1731
✉ Neilson-Hays Library, 195 Th Surawong ⏱ Tue, Thu, Fri & Sat 9.30am-4pm, Wed 9.30am-5pm, Sun 9.30am-2pm
🚇 Chong Nonsi 🚌 1, 16, 35, 36, 75, 93 ♿ fair

Silpakorn Art Gallery

(3, B4) Silpakorn University is renowned for its exceptional Fine Arts Department, considered the best in Bangkok. Keep an eye on the press listings for upcoming temporary exhibitions and take a look through the excellent art bookshop next door.
☎ 0 2221 5874/5
✉ 31 Th Na Phra Lan ⏱ Mon-Fri 9am-7pm, Sat 10am-5pm
🚌 503, 506, 508, 12, 44 🚢 Tha Chang ♿ fair

Tadu Contemporary Art

(2, C4) One of the major nexus of art, culture and conversation, Tadu focuses on contemporary exhibits, theatre, dance and avant-garde performances. It also collaborates with various film organisations promoting Thai cinema.
☎ 0 2645 2473 ✉ 99/2 Th Tiamruammit, Barcelona Motors Bldg, 7th fl
⏱ Mon-Sat 10am-6pm
🚌 taxi ♿ good

Thavibu Gallery (4, B5)

Young and irreverent artists from Southeast Asia (namely Burma, Thailand and Vietnam) are showcased in this virtual and tangible gallery. With a huge Internet presence, Thavibu cultivates a wide international audience and is a major resource for the region.
☎ 0 2266 5454
💻 www.thavibu.com
✉ 91 9/1 Th Silom, 3rd fl, Silom Galleria
⏱ Tue-Sat 11am-7pm, Sun noon-6pm 🚌 502, 504, 505 ♿ good

Contemporary creations to surprise and sustain you: Silpakorn Art Gallery

NOTABLE BUILDINGS

Baiyoke Sky Hotel (2, B4)

It's a bird; it's a crane; no, it's the Baiyoke Sky Hotel, the nation's tallest scraper. At a gangly 88 storeys (309m tall), the Baiyoke is visible from every corner of the city, and once it passes out of sight you've stumbled into the provinces.

☎ 0 2656 3000
✉ 222 Th Ratchaprarop
$ observatory 200B
🕐 10.30am-10.30pm
🚇 Phayathai
🚌 504, 513 ♿ good

Bank of Asia (4, C6)

During the crazy '80s, when no building project was too outlandish or expensive, architect Sumet Jumsai created his now-famous 'robot building' for the Bank of Asia. Few were keen on it at the time, but now it seems quaint and retro. It is best viewed from the Chong Nonsi Skytrain platform.

✉ cnr Th Sathon Tai & Soi Pikun
🕐 closed to the public
🚇 Chong Nonsi

Chitlada Palace (3, F1)

Rama V, Queen Sirikit and some royal white elephants live at Chitlada Palace, but, obviously, it's not open to the public. It's actually pretty difficult to spot the palace proper but you will spy an unusual sight in Bangkok – rice paddies and animal pastures (part of the king's agricultural projects) from outside the fence.

✉ cnr Th Ratchawithi & Th Phra Ram V, Dusit
🕐 closed to the public
🚌 503, 510

Democracy Monument (3, C4)

Four-pronged Democracy Monument holds a key place in Bangkok's political history. Built to commemorate the nation's transition from absolute monarchy to constitutional monarchy in 1932, the monument is the natural home of pro-democracy rallies, including the tragic demonstrations of 1992 that turned bloody at the hands of the military.

✉ cnr Th Ratchadamnoen Klang & Th Din So
$ free 🚌 511, 512, 44
⛴ Tha Phra Athit (Banglamphu) ♿ good

Hualamphong Station (3, F7)

In the tradition of European train stations, Hualamphong is more than just a terminus for the national rail lines; it is a signature of the prevailing architectural style, known as Thai Art Deco. Emerging after WWI, Thai Art Deco borrowed from the European style with a vaulted iron roof and neoclassical portico, while the two-toned skylights exemplify pure De Stijl Dutch modernism.

✉ Th Phra Ram IV
🚌 501, 507, 53, 73
Ⓜ Hualamphong
♿ good

No competition: Baiyoke Sky Hotel

White knight defending the City of Angels: Phra Sumen Fort

Old Customs House (3, E9)

Outfitted in pompous columns and transom windows, the Old Customs House faces Mae Nam Chao Phraya, Bangkok's former front-door to the world. Built in the 1880s, this crumbling monument now houses the fire brigade and is hauntingly beautiful as its shutters sag from neglect and laundry flaps in the unpainted balconies.
✉ **Soi 36, Th Charoen Krung** ☽ **closed to the** public 🚌 **75, 115**
⚓ **Tha Oriental**

Oriental Hotel (3, E9)

Quite simply, the Oriental (p95) is the most famous hotel in Bangkok, having played tropical pit stop to Joseph Conrad, Noel Coward, Graham Greene, Gore Vidal and Barbara Cartland. The days of steamship travel are easily evoked in the white-shuttered, colonial-style Author's Lounge (p79) or the Bamboo Bar (p89).

The hotel has a dress code (no backpacks, no sandals and no shorts).
☎ **0 2236 0400**
✉ **48 Soi Oriental, Th Charoen Krung**
☽ **variable** 🚇 **Saphan Taksin** 🚌 **75, 115** ⚓ **Tha Oriental or hotel shuttle boat from Tha Sathon**
♿ **good**

Phra Sumen Fort (6, B1)

Rock-solid and blindingly white, Phra Sumen Fort in Santichaiprakan Park is one of Banglamphu's most recognisable landmarks. Built in 1783, the imposing octagonal building was one of many fortresses along Khlong Banglamphu designed to defend the city against invasion. These days, it's a passive observer to the traveller onslaught of Banglamphu.
✉ **cnr Th Phra Athit & Th Phra Sumen**
$ **free** 🚌 **506, 53**
⚓ **Tha Phra Athit (Banglamphu)**
♿ **good**

Sample steamship Siam with tea in the Author's Lounge (p79) at the Oriental Hotel

PARKS & GARDENS

Some Bangkok residents confess to the odd fantasy of rolling on a patch of lawn, such is the pitiful amount of park space in the city. At least the few parks are well utilised, whether it's for aerobics classes, family gatherings or marketplaces.

Benchasiri Park (5, D2)
In summer, this park, built to honour Queen Sirikit's 60th birthday, hosts many open-air events. It's built around an ornamental lake, with most of the surrounding lawn space taken by canoodling couples and teenage mating rituals-in-progress. If you're lucky you might spy a *tàkrâw* game.
✉ btwn Sois 22 & 24, Th Sukhumvit ⏲ 5am-8pm $ free ⛾ Phrom Phong ♿ excellent

Chatuchak Park (2, B3)
Most people visit this park unintentionally — one of its corners is devoted to the Chatuchak Weekend Market — but it is worth a Skytrain trip for some solitude. There's a big kids' playground and sculptures are dotted throughout its vast grounds.
✉ Th Kamphaeng Phet $ free ⏲ 5am-8pm ⛾ Mo Chit subway Chatuchak Park ♿ excellent

Sanam Luang (6, A3)
Lumphini Park may be the green heart of Bangkok but Sanam Luang (Royal Field) is its ceremonial soul. Cremations of members of the royal family (including many from the present Chakri dynasty) and the annual May ploughing ceremony (see p84), which kicks off the rice-growing

Standing on ceremony: leisure time at ceremonial Sanam Luang

season, are held here at Sanam Luang.
✉ bordered by Th Na Phra That, Th Na Phra Lan, Th Ratchadamnoen Nai, Th Somdet Phra Pin Klao $ free ⏲ 5am-8pm ⛴ Tha Chang ♿ good

Santichaiprakan Park (6, B1)
It's a tiny patch of greenery interspersed with much concrete but somehow this park has got a soul. Every evening, it's bustling with families, travellers attempting circus tricks and an amusing open-air aerobics class. The riverside pathway, heading (and gradually being expanded) southwards, makes for a serene promenade. The neighbourhood's only remaining *lamphu* trees (for which Banglamphu derives its name) reside here.
✉ cnr Th Phra Athit & Th Phra Sumen $ free ⏲ 5am-8pm ⛌ 506, 53 ⛴ Tha Phra Athit (Banglamphu) ♿ good

Kite Fights
During kite-fighting season, between February and April, the skies above Sanam Luang become dangerous, hotly contested territory. Fights are held between many teams, who fly either a 'male' or 'female' kite and are assigned a particular territory, winning points if they can force a competitor into their zone.

QUIRKY BANGKOK

Bangkok itself is one big quirky attraction. But there's plenty that stands out as particularly curious, even after you've seen the snake-blood stalls at Lumphini Park.

House of Gems (3, F9)

The name 'House of Gems' is an interesting sales pitch for a shop claiming to sell dinosaur droppings. If you look in the window, dry cross-sections will teach you the subtle difference between the 'gems' of a carnivorous dinosaur, compared to its herbivorous friends. Don't say we didn't tell you that there's nothing you can't buy in Bangkok.

✉ 1218 Th Charoen Krung, near Th Surawong ☼ 10am-6pm Mon-Sat 🚌 75, 115, 116 🚢 Tha Oriental ☒ fair

Lingam (Phallus) Shrine (4, G1)

This little shrine at the back of Raffles Nai Lert Park was built for the spirit of a nearby tree. But then all these wooden phalluses started appearing, so that it's now like a dense wooden penis forest. Many women come to the shrine to pray for fertility.

✉ Nai Lert Park, Th Withayu ☼ 8am-6pm 💲 free 🚢 khlong taxi to Tha Withayu ☒ limited

Museum of Forensic Medicine (3, A3)

Seriously, do not come to this museum with a full stomach or if the slightest drop of blood makes you faint. It has preserved body parts that have been crushed, shot, stabbed and raped, with grisly before-and-after photos, as well as

the entire remains of a notorious Thai murderer. The small shrines next to babies' remains are sobering.

☎ 0 2419 7000 ✉ 2nd fl, Forensic Pathology Bldg, Siriraj Hospital, Th Phran-nok, Thonburi 💲 40B ☼ Mon-Fri 8.30am-4.30pm 🚢 Tha Rot Fai ☒ good

Queen Saovabha Memorial Institute (7, B1)

This snake farm, one of only a few worldwide, was established in 1923 to breed snakes for antivenenes. The snake shows are a nice sideline, where snake handlers educate and freak out visitors about snakes by letting the baddest ones loose (don't fret, you're safe in the stands).

☎ 0 2252 0161 ✉ cnr Th Phra Ram IV & Th Henri Dunant 💲 70B ☼ Mon-Fri 8.30am-4.30pm, Sat & Sun 8.30am-noon; shows Mon-Fri 11am & 2.30pm, Sat & Sun 11am 🚌 Sala Daeng Ⓜ Samyen ☒ good

Trok Itsaranuphap (3, D7)

Nudge your way deep into one of Chinatown's famous capillaries, where a 200-year-old day market (Talat Gao) peddles dried goods, half-alive filleted fish and vats of unidentifiable pickled things. The soi's poetic finale is lined with stalls selling elaborate funeral offerings. Along the way it changes names to Soi 16 and Soi 21.

✉ Trok Itsaranuphap from Sampeng Lane (Soi Wanit 1) to Th Yommarat Sukhum ☼ 6am-6pm 💲 free 🚢 Tha Ratchawong ☒ fair

Can you handle it? A handler and his King Cobra at the Queen Saovabha Memorial Institute (Snake Farm).

BANGKOK FOR CHILDREN

During kite-flying season, head for the parks and the action of the skies. But when it's hot and humid and the kids are cranky, your best option is probably one of the many air-conditioned shopping centres with amusements galore.

Central World Ice Skating (4, F1) You will feel like you're in the 'burbs, or at least an American teen movie, at this ice-skating rink at the very top of the World Trade Centre. It's a functional rink with no frills but lots of corny music.
✉ 7th fl, Central World Plaza, cnr Th Phra Ram I & Th Ratchadamri ⏰ Mon-Fri 10am-8.30pm, Sat & Sun 10am-2.45pm & 3.30-8.30pm 💲 150B 🚇 Chitlom 🛶 *khlong* taxi to Tha Pratunam ♿ good

Children's Discovery Museum (2, B3) Through hands-on activities, learning is well disguised as fun. Kids can stand inside a bubble or see how an engine works. Most activities are geared

to children aged five to ten. There is also a toddler-suitable playground at the back of the main building.
☎ 0 2615 7333 ✉ Queen Sirikit Park, Th Kamphaeng Phet 4, opposite Chatuchak Weekend Market ⏰ 9am-5pm Tue-Fri, 10am-6pm Sat & Sun 💲 70/50B 🚇 Mo Chit subway Chatuchak Park ♿ good

Dusit Zoo (3, E2) It would be easy to spend a day here. The peaceful grounds of this zoo, which once hosted the royal botanical garden, have a plethora of eateries as well as a playground and a big lake for paddle-boating. The animal-housing areas are not the most modern.
☎ 0 2281 2000 ✉ Th Phra Ram V, btwn Th

Ratchawithi & Th Sri Ayuthaya 💲 50/30B ⏰ 9am-6pm 🚌 510, 18 ⚓ Tha Thewet ♿ excellent

Jamboree (5, D2) A corner of this glamorous shopping centre is for the rug rats. There's a gym-style playground, coin-operated Godzillas to ride, child-sized cars to drive plus loads of video games.
☎ 0 2664 8000 ✉ 3rd fl, the Emporium, btwn Sois 22 & 24 ⏰ Mon-Fri 10.30am-10pm, Sat & Sun 10am-10pm 🚇 Phrom Phong ♿ good

Planetarium & Museum of Science (5, F2) The best thing about the Planetarium & Museum of Science is the emphasis

The loving touch: mural at Dusit Zoo painted by local children

Babysitters

It might be hard finding a babysitter if you're not staying in one of the better hotels – most Bangkok residents use extended family or maids rather than a babysitter – but few places will bat an eyelid if you bring the kids with you. The Australian-New Zealand Women's Group recommends **Ramida's Babysitting Services** (☎ 0 2634 7163).

on hands-on involvement. The exhibits aren't wildly exciting or well-maintained, but are interesting enough to spend an hour on. Get an insight into how Thais interpret the skies during a planetarium show (Tue 10am in English for groups with reservations).
☎ 0 2392 5952 ⊠ Th Sukhumvit, btwn Sois 40 & 42 $ 40/20B ☼ Tue-Sun 8.30am-4.30pm 🚇 Ekamai ♿ fair

Safari World Safari World bills itself as the 'World of Happiness'. It's undoubtedly fun and you do get two top attractions at this vast wildlife centre: the drive-through Safari Park, with African and Asian animals, and walk-through Marine Park, with dolphin shows, which could certainly make you happy. Set aside a day to see everything in this open-air zoo.
☎ 0 2518 1000 🖥 www.safariworld .com ⊠ 99 Th Ramindra, Minburi $ 700/450B ☼ 9am-5pm 🚌 27 from Victory Monument, then *săwngthăew* (small pick-up truck) ♿ good

SF City Bowl (4, D2) Thai teenagers crowd this psychedelically decorated

bowling alley at all hours of the day and night. The cost varies, depending what time of the day you play.
☎ 0 2611 7171 ⊠ 7th fl, Mah Boon Krong, cnr Th Phra Ram I & Th Phayathai $ 70-90B ☼ 10am-1am 🚇 National Stadium ♿ good

Siam Park You'll probably be fighting to have the first go on some of the

Siam Center (p55)

waterslides, which come in all shapes and sizes. If your kids are big then leave them to the slides or amusement rides while you kick back on the artificial beach complete with not-so-gnarly 'surf'.
☎ 0 2919 7200 🖥 www.siamparkcity .com, in Thai ⊠ Th Ramindra, Minburi $ 400/300B ☼ Mon-Fri 10am-6pm, Sat & Sun 10am-7pm 🚌 27 from Victory Monument ♿ good

Sports Zone (4, D2) Got teenagers who are just too cool for you? Well then banish them to this teen paradise, where gangs of kids packed into glass-encased karaoke booths satisfy their basketball jones in mini-courts or smile for the camera in those sticker-photo booths.
⊠ 4th fl, Siam Center, cnr Th Phayathai & Th Phra Ram I $ variable ☼ 10am-9pm 🚇 Siam Square ♿ good

Wat Prayoon (3, C7) Near the old Portuguese quarter in Thonburi is this unusual temple complex. An artificial hill, built under the orders of Rama III, is littered with curious miniature shrines, and little temples. Fruit vendors sell snacks for children to feed to the resident turtles.
⊠ 24 Th Prachadhipok cnr Th Thetsaban Sai 1, beside Memorial Bridge $ free ☼ 8am-6pm ⛴ cross-river ferry from Tha Pak Talaad (Atsadang) ♿ good

MEDITATION COURSES

Short- or long-term meditation instruction is available to foreign visitors at temples and retreat centres throughout Thailand. English proficiency of the teachers ranges from adequate to excellent. You'll be expected to wear white robes (available from nearby religious shops) when studying meditation at a temple. You should also attend the opening ceremony, where you should provide offerings of incense, candles or fruit to your teacher and the closing ceremony, at which you formally thank your teacher. The concept of respect for your teacher is of paramount importance.

Vipassana Meditation Section (3, B4) Twice a month, lectures in English on Buddhism are held at Maha Chulalongkorn Rajavidyalaya, a Buddhist university and Southeast Asia's most important place of Buddhist study.
☎ 0 2623 5881 ✉ Mahachula Bldg, Maha Chulalongkorn Rajavidyalaya University, Wat Mahathat
💲 free ☼ 3-5pm every 2nd & 4th Sat
🚌 503, 506, 53
🚲 Tha Chang ♿ fair

Wat Mahathat (3, B4) Wat Mahathat's International Buddhist Meditation Centre is where most Westerners study *satipatthana* (mindfulness) meditation in Bangkok. Classes are held three times daily. Accommodation is available on the temple grounds to male and female trainees provided they follow the strict regulations.
☎ 0 2222 6011 ✉ Section 5, Wat Mahathat 3, Th Maharat 💲 donations accepted ☼ 7am, 1pm,

6pm 🚌 503, 506, 53
🚲 Tha Maharat ♿ fair

World Fellowship of Buddhists (5, D2) On the first Sunday of the month, this centre of Theravada Buddhism hosts meditation classes in English from 2pm to 5.30pm. The fellowship also holds interesting forums on Buddhist issues.
☎ 0 2661 1284
🖥 www.wfb-hq.org
✉ Benjasiri Park, Soi 24, Th Sukhumvit 💲 free
🚇 Phrom Phong ♿ fair

THAI COOKING SCHOOLS

Benjarong Restaurant at Dusit Thani (7, C2) If you haven't had a rowdy night, you could try the Saturday morning classes run by the Benjarong restaurant's head chef. The classes, taken individually or as part of a 12-part course, are based on dishes served at the restaurant. Best of all, you eat your creations for lunch.
☎ 0 2236 3600 ✉ Dusit Thani, cnr Th Silom & Th Phra Ram IV, Silom
💲 US$180 🚇 Sala Daeng

Mrs Balbir's Restaurant (5, B2) In between running her restaurant (p73) and hosting a cooking show,

Mrs Balbir teaches Thai cooking on Fridays. Private lessons, children's classes and tours to fresh-produce markets are also available.
☎ 0 2651 0498
🖥 www.mrsbalbir.com
✉ 155/18 Soi 11/1, Th Sukhumvit
💲 450-550B 🚇 Nana

Nipa Thai Restaurant at Landmark Hotel (5, A2) Get a copy of the lesson program at this top-notch restaurant and select just the days in the week-long course that feature dishes you fancy. All students get a free spice box, recipe book and meal at the restaurant.

☎ 0 2254 0404 ✉ btwn Sois 4 & 6, Th Sukhumvit
💲 US$100 🚇 Nana

Oriental Hotel Cooking Centre (3, E9) Avid chefs might find the hands-off approach frustrating but you learn a lot by watching. Daily classes are held as well as longer courses including classes, meals, accommodation, spa sessions and limousine transfers.
☎ 0 2437 6211 🖥 www .mandarinoriental.com
✉ 48 Th Oriental
💲 US$150 🚲 free shuttle boat from Oriental Hotel

TRADITIONAL MASSAGE

There is no shortage of massage shops in Bangkok, but not all are created equally. Some blur the line between ancient massage and 'recreation', while others are massage assembly-lines with a constant stream of prostrate bodies. But as a *Farang* article once pointed out, massage is like pizza – when it is bad, it is still good. The going rate is 300B for 1 hour of foot or body massage and 500B for an oil massage.

Buathip Thai Massage (5, A2) Buathip has long been known for its blind masseuses, who will give you a strong and intuitive treatment. It's a low-key place favoured by Thai regulars and expats.
☎ 0 2251 2627
✉ 4/1-2 Soi 5, Th Sukhumvit ☼ 10am-midnight
🚇 Nana ♿ good

Marble House (7, B2) Don't worry that Marble House is in the middle of the sleazy Thaniya scene. The work of its traditional masseurs is so highly respected that it doesn't need to sell sex. Its air-conditioned teak rooms make the massages even more restorative.
☎ 0 2235 3529
✉ 37/18-19 Soi Surawong Plaza, Th Surawong, Silom
☼ 10am-midnight
🚇 Sala Daeng ♿ good

Ruen-Nuad Massage (7, B3) A little more spa-style than the typical parlour shopfront, Ruen-Nuad has deceptively strong masseuses who will fret your pressure points and flush out those stagnant energy pools.
☎ 0 2632 2662
✉ 42 Th Convent, Th Silom ☼ 10am-10pm
🚇 Sala Daeng ♿ fair

Genuine Thai massage in Thaniya

Wat Pho Massage School (3, B6) The primary training school for Thai massage also has a drop-in centre for exhausted sightseers needing a little kneading. If impressed by their work, you might consider enrolling in one of five two-week classes on different aspects of this traditional art; former participants say that the massage classes are strong on technique but weak on theory.
☎ 0 2221 3686 ✉ Soi Penphat (not signed), Th Maharat ☼ 8am-5pm
🚌 501, 507, 508
⚓ Tha Tien ♿ limited

Thai Massage

You've put your cotton pyjamas on and you've lain down on the mattress, which is on a raised wooden platform. What next? Something that's like a cross between a yoga session, reflexology massage and a workout with the chiropractor. Thais take their massage seriously and consider it an important part of holistic health, using it to relax and prevent disease.

DAY SPAS

Banyan Tree Spa (4, F5)

You wind your way along pebbled pathways to your private spa suite, in a traditional Thai design and decorated with floating orchid bowls and carvings. The Balinese Boreh is the luxurious treatment of choice – you are treated to 3 hours of deep-tissue massage, a body 'wrap' in warming spices and then a carrot rub.

☎ 0 2679 1052
🖥 www.banyantree.com
✉ 20th & 21st fls, Banyan Tree, 21/100 Th Sathon Tai
🕑 9am-10pm 🚇 Sala Daeng 🚌 15 ♿ good

Grande Spa & Fitness Club (5, B2)

The Sheraton's spa is small, dark and intimate, with low roofs. Each of the 11 teak rooms, including a few massage suites for couples, is self-contained, with a shower and dressing room. Loll back in one of the cavernous hydrotherapy baths and detox to your heart's content.

☎ 0 2653 0333
🖥 www.luxury collection.com/grandesuk humvit ✉ Sheraton Grande Sukhumvit, 250 Th Sukhumvit, btwn Sois 12 & 14 🕑 8am-10pm 🚇 Asoke ♿ good

Oriental Spa Thai Health & Beauty Centre (3, E9)

When jetlag hits, you have no option but to call in the Revitaliser, this spa's legendary treatment which pummels, rubs and soothes the nasties from your system and turns you into a human being again. When it opened in 1993, the Oriental was Thailand's first spa and it has won countless prestigious awards since then.

☎ 0 2439 7613
🖥 www.mandarin oriental.com

✉ Oriental Hotel, 48 Soi Oriental, Th Charoen Krung
🕑 9am-10pm
🚢 free shuttle from Oriental Hotel
♿ good

Oriental Spa Thai Health & Beauty Centre

Dreaming of a Hospital Vacation?

Medical tourism, an apparent oxymoron, is a booming business here. Bangkok's hospitals are on par with Western facilities and cover all the bases – including dentistry, nips and tucks, corrective surgeries or sex changes – for less than the price at home.

At the top of the list, **Bumrungrad Hospital** (4, H2; ☎ 0 2667 1000; www.bum rungrad.com; 33 Soi 3, Th Sukhumvit; 🚇 Nana) has five-star service, is US-managed and -accredited and caters mainly to foreigners. **BNH** (7, C3; ☎ 0 2632 0550; www.bnhhospital.com; Th Convent) is also well-regarded for general medicine. **Dental Hospital** (☎ 02 2260 5000; 88/88 Soi 49, Th Sukhumvit) is a private dental clinic with fluent-English-speaking dentists. **Bangkok Dental Spa** (☎ 02 651-080727; Methawattana Building, 2nd floor, Soi 19, Th Sukhumvit) combines oral hygiene with spa services (foot and body massage).

For every Tom, Dick and Harry who'd rather be Jane, **Yanhee Hospital** (2, A3; ☎ 0 2879 0300; www.yanhee.net; Th Charoen Sanit Wong, near Phra Ram VII bridge) provides sex reassignment and chondroplasty (shaving of the Adam's apple).

Out & About

WALKING TOURS
Chinatown to Little India

Wade into the back alleys of Chinatown and Little India (Phahurat). From Tha Ratchawong ferry stop, follow Th Ratchawong and turn right on to the tail-end of Sampeng Lane. Turn left at **Trok Itsaranuphap** (**1**; p38), strangled by a sense-assaulting **market** (**2**; p55). Cross Th Yaowarat and grab a snack from either **Hong Kong Noodles** or **Hong Kong Dim Sum** (**3**; p70), across from a 'fresh' meat market. At Charoen Krung, detour to **Wat Mangkon Kamalawat** (**4**; p28), before rebounding to the alley now mellowed by **funerary shops** (**5**; p38). Then circle back to Th Yaowarat by taking a right on to Th Phla Phla Chai and another

Th Phahurat in Little India

right onto Th Plaengnam. Follow Th Yaowarat to Th Ratchawong and turn left, then right on to **Sampeng Lane** (**6**; p57). Follow it all the way to Phahurat. Across Th Chakraphet is fabric-filled **Phahurat Market** (**7**; p56) and to the left is **Sri Gurusingh Sabha Temple** (**8**; p27). Wrap up this sweaty ramble at air-conditioned **Old Siam Plaza**'s (**9**; p70) dessert emporium.

Get shirty at Phahurat Market (p56)

> **distance** 3.4km **duration** 2hr
> ▶ **start** ⚓ Tha Ratchawong
> ● **end** 🚌 53

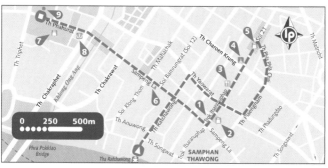

Ko Ratanakosin

Explore Thailand's spiritual core on this morning procession. Strict dress codes are enforced at most temples. Start at Tha Chang ferry stop and take Th Na Phra Lan along the white-washed walls of the **Grand Palace** and **Wat Phra Kaew** (**1**; pp8-9) to the third gate (go directly into the complex; ignore the touts). After visiting the wat, turn right and cross Th Sanamchai, which runs along beside Sanam Luang (p37), to the home of Bangkok's city spirit, **City Pillar** (**2**; p27). Go south down Th Sanamchai for 500m and then turn right onto Th Chetuphon, where you will enter **Wat Pho** (**3**; p10), Bangkok's oldest temple. If your feet are aching, head towards **Wat Pho's massage school** (**4**; p42). Take Th Maharat north to Th Thai Wang and turn left to catch the cross-river ferry to **Wat Arun** (**5**; p11). Back in Bangkok, head up Th Maharat and briefly detour to Th Na Phra Lan to hit **Silpakorn Art Gallery** (**6**; p34) or eat at **Krisa Coffee Shop** (**7**; p69). Now recharged, backtrack to Th Maharat with **Wat Mahathat** (**8**; p26) on your right and the **amulet market** (**9**; p55) on either side.

Money can buy you auspicious amulets

distance 2.4km **duration** 2hr
▶ **start** ⚓ Tha Chang
● **end** ⚓ Tha Maharat

That's what we call detail: Wat Arun's *praang*

Wat Saket to Pak Khlong Market

Ramble through this sleepy neighbourhood of temples, crumbling neo-classical buildings and cottage industries. From Tha Phan Fah, follow Th Boriphat over the bridge to **Wat Saket's Golden Mount** (**1**; p18), for a

Vegetable of fire

distance 1.7km **duration** 1½hr
▶ **start** 🚣 Tha Phan Fah
(*khlong* taxi)
● **end** 🚣 Tha Ratchini
(river express)

breezy view of Bangkok's skyline. Continue down Th Boriphat and cross Th Bamrung Muang, past an **old woodworking centre** (**2**) for teak furniture and decorations. Take the first *soi* on your left into the **Monk Bowl Village** (**3**; p31), another craft village that hand-hammers alms bowls. Back on Th Boriphat, turn right on to Th Luang and cut through shady **Romaneenart Park** (**4**) to Th Siri Phong, where you'll turn right. At the next intersection, a graceful red arch forms the **Giant Swing** (**5**; p29). Turn left on to Th Botphram passing **Wat Suthat** (**6**; p29) and a dense block of **religious shops** (**7**) selling Buddha figures and devotional items. At Khlong Lawt, one of the city's original canals, you can cross it and continue straight to follow the Ko Ratanakosin tour (p45) or follow Th Atsadang south to the flowers of **Pak Khlong Market** (**8**; p55).

Forged in the flames: monks' alms bowls

Old Banglamphu

Wander down Th Phra Athit, crowded with Ratanakosin-era mansions. To the right is **Ban Maliwan** (**1**), which now holds the offices of UN Food & Agriculture Organization. Backtrack to the impressive **Buddhist Society of Thailand** (**2**), on your left, and **Ban Phra Athit** (**3**), on your right. As a commoner, you can only glimpse gabled rooflines and shuttered windows just past the guarded gates. Soon the imposing white Phra Sumen Fort (p36) and the surrounding **Santichaiprakan Park** (**4**; p37) loom into view. Stop by **Roti Mataba** (**5**; p69) for a lunch-time snack.

Cross the busy intersection with Th Samsen and Th Chakraphong, where a right turn would lead you to the backpacker strip of Th Khao San (p86). On the right, the long white wall of **Wat Bowonniwet** (**6**; p28) signals the approach to a section of the **old city gate** (**7**). This part of Th Phra Sumen is lined with nationalistic shops selling Thai flags and Thai royal family paraphernalia ('We Love the King' bumper stickers). Turn right on Th Din So past the old shophouses all the way to the boldly modern **Democracy Monument** (**8**; p35).

You'll flip for the roti at Roti Mataba (p69)

distance 1.8km **duration** 1hr
- ▶ **start** 🚢 Tha Phra Athit (Banglamphu)
- ● **end** Democracy Monument
- 🚌 503, 506

Best defence: Phra Sumen Fort (p36)

DAY TRIPS
Ayuthaya
(1, B1)

During its heyday, Ayuthaya, capital of Siam, was one of Southeast Asia's most sophisticated – and, reputedly, glittering – cities. But a thorough sacking by the Burmese abruptly ended that golden age, leaving Ayuthaya in ruins. Today you can wander among the temple remnants that make up this Unesco World Heritage site, with the help of a hired bicycle (50B a day), *túk-túk* or *săwngthăew* (200B per hour).

Wat Phra Mahathat (30B) has an impressive *praang* (corn-cob-shaped stupa), while **Wat Ratburana** (30B) has a *chedi* (stupa) in the Singhalese style. **Wat Phra Si Sanphet** (30B) was the biggest temple of its time, as its three striking *chedi* in the classic Ayuthaya style will remind you. **Wat Yai Chai Mongkhon**'s (20B) reclining Buddha has graced many a postcard.

> **INFORMATION**
> *85km north of Bangkok*
> 🚌 from Bangkok's Hualamphong station (20B 3rd class; 1½ hr; every 30 min)
> 🕑 temple ruins 8am-6.30pm
> ℹ tourist office ☎ 035-246 076/7; 108/22 Th Si Sanphet; open 9am-5pm
> 🍴 Hua Raw Night Market & Chao Phrom Day Market, Th U Thong

In the evenings, many ruin-hoppers take a semicircle **boat ride** (400B, arranged at guesthouses) around the island with stops at **Wat Phanan Choeng** (20B) and **Wat Chai Wattanaram** (free), just in time to capture the setting sun amid the Ayuthaya-style ruins. The boat ride winds through the riverside communities where meals are cooked, dishes are washed, and conversations and TV sound effects waft from the banks. The trip ends at the night market, a fixture in the lives of the ancient city's citizens.

The Elephant Walk

After a day of lugging people around, Ayuthaya's working elephants knock off around 5pm and begin their commute home to the elephant kraal via Th Si Sanphet and Th Chee Kun.

Wat Chai Wattanaram, main Khmer *praang* and four lesser *praang*, Ayuthaya Historical Park

Ko Samet (1, C3)

Bangkok's beachside playground is a T-bone shaped island of squeaky blonde beaches, glassy water and not a single high-rise – all in all, surprisingly rustic considering its proximity to the capital. Despite its *au natural* demeanour, Ko Samet sits solidly on the beaten track with weekend crowds, jet skis, speedboats, nightly discos, sarong-sellers and beach masseuses. But footpaths skirting the rocky exterior provide mental, if not physical, seclusion.

INFORMATION

200km southeast of Bangkok

- 🚌 from Bangkok's Ekamai station (5, F2; 117B; 2½ hr; hourly) to Rayong, then *săwngthăew* (15B; 30 mins; frequent) to Ban Phe, then ferry to Ko Samet (50B; 45 min; hourly)
- 💲 200B entrance fee
- 🍽 Naga Bakery (☎ 0 3864 4035; Ao Hin Khok)

Consider walking the planks at Ao Cho

Designated a national park in 1981, Ko Samet was the scene of the Thai poet Sunthorn Phu's epic *Phra Aphaimani*, about a prince exiled to an undersea kingdom. A mermaid helps the prince escape to Ko Samet – a scene immortalised with a statue built on a rocky point separating Ao Hin Khok and Hat Sai Kaew.

Most boats from the mainland arrive at Na Dan pier, a short walk west of the widest and most popular stretch of sand, **Hat Sai Kaew** (Diamond Beach). Around the next headland are scruffy **Ao Hin Khok** and **Ao Phai**, fittingly claimed by backpackers and bars. **Ao Phutsa** is a nice little curve of sand before a lengthy run of rocky headlands leading to **Ao Wong Deuan**, a beach that resembles the girlie-bar scene of Pattaya, and **Ao Thian** (Candlelight Beach), claimed by Thai college kids and all-night guitar jams. Accommodation can be found at **Samed Villa** (☎ 0 3864 4094; Ao Phai; 2000B) and **Sai Kaew Villa** (☎ 0 3864 4144; Hat Sai Kaew; 600-1000B).

I can't believe I didn't bring my sunglasses

Damnoen Saduak Floating Market (1, A2)

Thailand's famous floating markets – women in straw hats and blue shirts paddling wooden boats laden with fresh produce and flowers – survive today for the tourists, not the locals. You can still catch a glimmer of the floating markets' former glory at **Damnoen Saduak**, but you have to arrive the night before so as to catch the market before the arrival of package tourists from Bangkok. Sounds like too much hassle? Then come when you can and enjoy what it has become - a floating souvenir market. You can also hire long-tails for exploration into the neighbouring *khlong* to see stilt houses, floating gas stations and small family businesses.

INFORMATION
80km southwest of Bangkok

🚌 from Bangkok's Southern bus terminal, air-con bus to Damnoen Saduak (65B; 2 hr; every 20 min from 6.30am)
🕐 4am-noon
🍴 floating noodle or fruit vendors

Amphawa Home-Stays (1, A2)

If you enjoy monk-like asceticism and can tip-toe through cultural differences, then an informal home-stay – organised by **Baan Song Thai Plai Pong Pang** (☎ 0 3475 7333) in the Amphawa district – connects you to the residents' riverine routines. You will awkwardly participate in daily customs such as morning offerings to the monks or walking plank pathways. The accommodation (a thin mattress on the floor) and the home-made meals are simple, but the immersion is complete. On certain lunar days, a floating market is held.

INFORMATION
70km southwest of Bangkok

🚌 from Bangkok's Southern bus terminal, air-con bus to Samut Songkhram (45B), blue local bus (10B) to Amphawa, motorcycle taxi to Baan Khok Ket
💲 350B for accommodation, 500B for longtail-boat hire

Movable feast: traders at the floating market, Damnoen Saduak

Ko Kret (2, A2)

Are your nerves shot from dodging *túk-túk* and withstanding earsplitting traffic? As soothing as a trip to a day spa, this island right in the middle of Mae Nam Chao Phraya is a crafty little getaway in every sense. Known for its distinctive pottery, Ko Kret receives relatively few visitors, although it's just a few hours from Bangkok. It's a laid-back island that you can walk around in a few hours as you're surveying the cottage pottery shops. This is Thailand's oldest settlement of Mon people, skilled potters originally from Burma.

INFORMATION

17km north of Bangkok

🛥 Tha Nonthaburi, then longtail (300B for 2 hr) to Ko Kret

✖ food stalls near the pier

Going potty, Ko Kret

Muang Boran (1, B2)

In the wrong hands, Muang Boran (Ancient City) could have been the Eurodisney of Thailand. But fortunately this enormous open-air museum was shaped by a philanthropist passionate about conserving Thailand's architectural traditions. It's such a genuinely wholesome place – all lush gardens, grazing wildlife, gushing streams and artisans at work. More than 100 mini-replicas of Thailand's important buildings – from temples to traditional houses – and monuments are spread over the 128ha site in the shape of Thailand. You could easily spend a day riding a bike (50B) around. The Folk Museum and its collection of traditional implements is worth a poke around to see how Thais once harvested their crops, wove cloth and managed their livestock.

INFORMATION

33km southeast of Bangkok

🚌 air-con 511 (16B) from Bangkok's Th Sukhumvit to Samat Prakan, then green bus 36 (6B)

☎ 0 2323 9253

🖳 www.ancientcity.com

✉ KM 33, old Th Sukhumvit

$ 100/50B

⏱ 8am-5pm

✖ floating market restaurant

A couch fit for a king at Muang Boran open-air museum

ORGANISED TOURS

Be careful of bogus tour operators – only book tours through travel agencies or operators with official licences from the Tourism Authority of Thailand (TAT).

ABC Amazing Bangkok Cyclists (5, D2) These popular bicycle trips transport city dwellers to Prakanong, in the southeast, where you can ride easily along narrow elevated walkways beside stilted houses and through fields and forests. The operators promise you won't spot a bit of traffic; all equipment is provided.
☎ 0 2712 9301
🖥 www.realasia.net
💲 1000B ⏱ 1-6pm

Manohra Rice Barge Dinner Cruise (2, A5) Dinner cruises in Bangkok are a dime a dozen, but this is one in a million – a restored rice barge, stunning food and the riverside temples lit up at night. There are also additional tours to Ayuthaya, including merit-making, candle-lit dinners and other ridiculously romantic activities.
☎ 0 2476 0022
🖥 www.manohra

cruises.com ✉ Bangkok Marriott Resort & Spa, 257 Th Charoen Nakhon, Thonburi 💲 from 1400B ⏱ 7.30-10pm

Chao Phraya River Express This company knows all the good spots along the river. Every Sunday tours cruise north to the Queen's Arts & Crafts Center and Bang Pa-In. And just as art fatigue sets in, the tour breaks the spell with a visit to the huge bird sanctuary at Wat Phai Lom.
☎ 0 2623 6001
🖥 www.chaophraya boat.com
✉ departs from Tha Maharat
💲 390/300B
⏱ 8am-6pm

Out of my way: barge across Mae Nam Chao Phraya

DIY Boat Tours

Escape the craziness by hiring a longtail to take you far, far away – to the Thonburi canals (Khlong Bangkok Noi and Khlong Bangkok Yai). You can make arrangements from Mit Chao Phraya's desk at Tha Chang (3, A5), where the going rate is around 400B an hour plus 20B mooring fee, or you can shop around at the other piers for a better price. Just make sure you're bargaining for an hourly rate rather than a per-person rate.

One of the best trips is along Khlong Bangkok Noi, which gradually changes from a congested city canal to a route lined with greenery, houses on stilts and Wat Suwannaram. This temple has exquisite *jataka* murals painted by two of early Bangkok's foremost religious muralists. Scenic Khlong Bangkok Yai travels past Wat Intharam, while Khlong Mon passes orchid farms.

Shopping

Even avowed anticonsumerism types weaken in Bangkok. One minute they're touting the virtues of a life without material possessions, the next they're admiring the fake Rolex on their wrist and finding out which Skytrain goes to Chatuchak. If you intend to launch a full-scale shopping assault, don't deny yourself a copy of the indispensable Nancy Chandler illustrated map of Bangkok, which is widely available.

DEPARTMENT STORES & SHOPPING CENTRES

Bangkok mall-rats have it good now that shopping centres have replaced parks as the public space of choice in this city starved of fresh air. There are loads of these mega-temples to consumerism – some even have bowling alleys, ice-skating rinks and fun-fairs.

Most shopping plazas are anchored by a department store (Tokyu, Zen, Sogo etc) that is worth pawing through during a sale or for sports equipment, but otherwise lack the sizzle of a Saks or Harvey Nics. (Plus the real people action is in the plaza thoroughfares or food courts.)

Central Chitlom (4, F2)
In this internationally educated department store, executive-strength credit cards cruise the escalators thumbing homewares, *faràng*-sized (Westerner-sized) clothes (look for Thai couture brand 'Tube') and cosmetics (look for Thai brand 'Erb').
☎ 0 2233 6930-9
✉ 1027 Th Ploenchit

⏰ 10am-9pm
🚇 Chitlom ♿ good

Gaysorn Plaza (4, F2)
This fashion palace entertains all the haughty international designers (Gucci, Prada, Vuitton et al) plus Thai fashion pioneers (Fly Now and Senada), giving credibility to the city's self-endowed title, 'Fashion City'. Also catering to all those naked walls in the City of Angels, the top-floor shops offer goods that can transform a home into a true showpiece with modern and antique Thai décor.
☎ 0 2656 1149 ✉ cnr Th Ploenchit & Th Rat-chadamri ⏰ 10am-10pm
🚇 Chitlom ♿ good

The Emporium (5, D2)
This top-flight mall cleverly woos young urban princesses and stately establishment queens by stocking the very hippest of fashion designers (Miu Miu, Prada), hardcore luxury brands (Chanel, Rolex) and classy eateries (Greyhound Café, Salon de l'Oriental). Despite the cat-walk sauntering of these high-society bag girls, it all comes together without a stitch of intimidation.
☎ 0 2664 8000 ✉ btwn Sois 22 & 24, Th Sukhumvit
⏰ 10.30am-10pm Mon-Fri, 10am-10pm Sat & Sun 🚇 Phrom Phong ♿ good

Wonderful wares in every nook and cranny of the Emporium

Four floors of the finest: River City shopping centre

Mah Boon Krong (4, D2)
Also known as MBK, this hyperactive mall smells like Thai teen spirit. Nearly all of the city's population under 20 can be found here on a more regular basis than they can in class or at home. Its seemingly endless floors of stalls and shops are the best place to buy contact lenses, mobile phones and good-looking knock-offs.
☎ 0 2217 9111 ✉ cnr Th Phra Ram I & Th Phayathai ⏱ 10am-10pm 🚇 National Stadium ♿ good

Panthip Plaza (4, E1)
Like a real-time version of eBay, Panthip is five floors of tech gear from legitimate hardware to flea-market surplus peripherals. True to Bangkok's lawless reputation, pirated software and DVD-encryption crackers shrug at that pesky notion of intellectual property.
☎ 0 2252 2783 ✉ Th Phetchaburi ⏱ 10am-8pm 🚌 505, 511, 512 ⛴ khlong taxi to Tha Pratunam ♿ limited

River City (4, A4) Only got time for one antique shop? Everything sold in this four-floor complex of art, antiques and auctioneers is the very best, whether it's a Burmese Buddha image, the finest black silk or a benjarong tea-set, and you pay for the quality. The stores can arrange to ship your buys back home.
☎ 0 2237 0077 ✉ Th Yotha off Th Charoen

Shopping Areas
Serious shoppers usually trawl the strip of Th Phra Ram I from Siam Square (3, C7) to the corner of Th Ratchadamri (3, C9). This boulevard of retail bliss is the home of the heavyweight shopping centres, like Mah Boon Krong (MBK), Siam Center and Siam Discovery Center. If your home currency is in good shape, you'll find sizzling bargains on Western brand names.

Then when their thoughts turn to Thai arts, crafts and antiques, they head down to the river and the rarefied air of River City (3, E8). Between here and the Oriental Hotel (4, A5), Th Charoen Krung and its offshoots boast craft shops. The soi off Th Sukhumvit (5, C2) are also worth checking out for little outlets of fabric, antiques, celadon and other craftworks, not to mention the Emporium shopping centre.

But the highlights for most shoppers are the markets, loud and crazy places where you can buy anything and everything. If it's not at the rambling, claustrophobic Chatuchak Weekend Market (2, B4), then it might not exist. To live like a local, elbow your way through the produce and product markets of Chinatown (3, D7) and Phahurat (3, C6). The best tourist markets – for that de rigueur fake handbag, watch or Western-sized clothing – are at Patpong (4, C5), Sukhumvit (5, B2) and Khao San (6, B3).

Fashion Sense

Think Bangkok's creatures of couture are slaves to the runways of the West? *Au contraire mon faràng*, Bangkok has a full house of local brands (Greyhound, Senada, Fly Now and Soda with retail outlets in Siam Center, Gaysorn Plaza or the Emporium) that combine city chic with Thai fabrics and sensibilities to produce clubwear, daywear and artwear. Of the high flyers, Chamnan Phakdeesuk of Fly Now has opened in London's Fashion Week twice, while Greyhound has created a lifestyle image of the 21st-century, *sànùk* (fun). Even the eternally unstylish Thai politicians have spotted a trend by naming Bangkok a 'Fashion City' in hopes that it will become a regional industry hub.

Krung ☒ 10am-10pm
🚌 75, 93 🚤 Tha Si
Phraya ☒ good

Siam Center & Siam Discovery Center (4, D2)
These sister centres – along with frenetic MBK – form Siam Square's shopping triumvirate. The Discovery Center boasts two floors stocked with eclectic and stylish home-furnishing stores integrating modular design. Follow the pouty, mobile-phone-wielding crowd to linked Siam Center, which is stuffed to the rafters with must-have, mid-range Thai labels.

Set to open in 2005, the affiliated Siam Paragon, located nearby, is intended to offer the same upmarket collection as the Emporium currently does.
☎ 0 2658 1000-19
✉ cnr Th Phayathai & Th Phra Ram I ☒ 10am-9pm
🚇 Siam ☒ good

MARKETS

Amulet Market (3, A4)
Thais wear amulets for protection, usually from evil spirits or bad fortune. Wat Ratchanadta's market is one of the most famous places in Bangkok to buy amulets, which are usually of Buddha images but often Hindu deities, Thai monks, and even phalluses to protect against infertility.
✉ several small *soi* off Th Maharat, across from Wat Mahathat ☒ 9am-5pm 🚌 508, 512, 53
🚤 Tha Maharat ☒ fair

Khao San Market (6, B3)
The traders here know their market so well – you've got the hair-braiders, the henna tattoos, the bootleg CD-makers, the hippy jewellery stalls and the

fake Birkenstocks plus an excellent range of clothes in big sizes. It's fun, lively and good value.
✉ Th Khao San
☒ 5-11pm 🚌 506, 53, 17
🚤 Tha Phra Athit (Banglamphu) ☒ good

Pak Khlong Market (3, C6) Get up early or stay out late to catch this

24-hour market at its most raucous, as the city stocks up on its orchids, lilies and other tropical flowers. Pak Khlong is Bangkok's biggest and most famous flower market, though it also has some good fruit and veggie stalls. Plans are slowly unfolding to convert this market into a tourist park. Where will the flowers go?

All smiles: we think her secret ingredient is actually chilli

Colours of the rainbow: something for everyone at Patpong night market

That part of the plan is still undecided.

✉ Th Chakkaphet, near Tha Ratchini, Phahurat
🕙 24hr 🚌 53
🚇 Tha Ratchini ♿ fair

Patpong Night Market (7, B2) The Patpong area is the ultimate Bangkok cliché where everything can be had for a price. In one corner are the famous circus-like sex shows and in the other is a crowded market selling knock-offs of every coveted brand name (make sure you bargain hard as prices are inflated). And lying in ambush are the 'DVD, CVD, Sex' video sellers who pop up just as your wife has stepped past.

✉ Sois 1 & 2, Th Silom
🕙 6pm-2am
🚇 Sala Daeng ♿ fair

Phahurat Market (3, C6) If your sense of direction is shocking, enter this warren of shops selling fabrics, haberdashery, Indian jewellery, samosas and saris at your peril. After a while, every little laneway within Little India's famous, labyrinthine market begins to look the same – more faux fur bolts of fabric and rowdy prints, Thai dance costumes and a heck of a lot of kids' stuff (pyjamas, jumpers, bibs).

✉ cnr Th Phahurat & Th Chakraphet 🕙 10am-9pm 🚌 73 🚇 Tha Saphan Phut ♿ fair

Pratunam Market (4, F1) Pratunam market is where the city's African community goes to shop. It sells a bit of everything and is the best stop for an extra piece of luggage, an umbrella and Cookie Monster slippers.

✉ cnr Th Phetchaburi & Th Ratchaprarop
🕙 10am-9pm
🚌 505, 511, 512
🚤 khlong taxi to Tha Pratunam ♿ fair

Faking It

Whether it's calling your shop Dairy Princess or copying a pair of Diesel cargo pants stitch for stitch, ripping off successful Western brands has become an art form in Bangkok. Seasoned market shoppers develop a keen eye for distinguishing between the good fake and the bad fake. And in the case of Levi's, which are produced in Thailand, the real deal occasionally and mysteriously appears at the markets, dirt cheap.

It's all highly illegal, of course, and many Western manufacturers have long been pressuring the Thai government to get these goods off the street, but, so far, to little effect.

Driving a Hard Bargain

Thais respect a good bargainer, someone who can get a reasonable price without either seller or buyer losing face. Here are some hints:

- do your homework on prices
- don't start bargaining unless you intend to buy
- always let the vendor make the first offer and then ask 'is that your best price?'
- don't be aggressive or raise your voice; be friendly
- remember that there's a fine line between bargaining and niggling – how much is 10B really worth to you, anyway?

Sampeng Market (3, D6)

You can get anything you want in Sampeng Lane as long as you appreciate the concept of economies of scale. Sandals? Take a 12-pack. Inflatable Superman? They've got five for 400B. If you look hard, you'll find some shopfronts selling tea and tobacco, just like in the old days.

✉ Soi Wanit 1 (Sampeng Lane) ⊙ 10am-10pm
🚌 501, 507, 73 ⚓ Tha Ratchawong ♿ fair

Soi Lalai Sap Market (7, A3)

Literally 'the *soi* that melts your money away', this street is jam-packed at lunchtime with Thai workers bargaining for fake handbags and other leather goods, homewares and clothing. It's just next to the Bangkok Bank on Th Silom. Rejects from brand-name factories in Cambodia sometimes make an appearance here.

✉ Soi 5, Th Silom
⊙ 10am-3pm Mon-Fri
🚇 Chong Nonsi 🚌 502, 504, 505, 15 ♿ fair

Sukhumvit Market (4, H3)

A market for the true fake aficionado, who knows the seriously big difference between a good *faux* Fendi handbag and one with dodgy stitching and a bum zip. Other must-haves include soccer kits, watches, sunglasses, penis-shaped lighters and naked lady ashtrays.

✉ btwn Sois 2 & 12, 3 & 15, Th Sukhumvit
⊙ 11am-10.30pm
🚇 Nana ♿ fair

Food stalls set up in the early evening on Soi 4 (Nana Tai), Sukhumvit

JEWELLERY & SILVERWARE

As one of the world's biggest exporters of gems and ornaments, Thailand offers some good buys in unset gems, especially jade, rubies and sapphires, and finished jewellery – but that's if you know what you're doing as there are lots of scams. If you can't tell blue glass from a sapphire, buy from reputable dealers. The shops we list here have been recommended by expatriates.

Johnny's Gems (3, C5)
Johnny's is consistently recommended by expats, who return again and again for the reliable set jewellery and attentive service.
☎ 0 2222 1756
✉ 199 Th Feuang Nakhon, Th Charoen Krung
🕐 10am-7pm
🚌 507, 508 🚤 Tha Tien 🚶 good

Lin Silvercraft (3, F9)
Lin might be a bit pricier than your average Bangkok silver shop but you know you're getting the genuine article. You can pick up classic pieces like silver chokers, thick bangles and custom-engraved cuff links.
☎ 0 2235 2108
✉ 14 Soi 40, Th Charoen Krung 🕐 10am-8pm
🚤 Saphan Taksin
🚌 75, 115, 116
🚤 Tha Oriental 🚶 good

SV Jewellery (3, F9)
With a big showroom on bustling Th Charoen Krung, SV Jewellery isn't just a shop for girly baubles and body decorations. You'll find cuff links in all sizes, shapes and attitudes, silver animals (including especially cute elephants) and homewares, like enormous gleaming photo frames and key rings.
☎ 0 2233 7347
✉ 1254-6 Th Charoen Krung 🕐 10am-5pm Mon-Sat 🚤 Saphan Taksin 🚌 75, 115, 116

🚤 Tha Oriental
🚶 fair

Uthai's Gems (4, G3)
You need to make an appointment to see Uthai's gems in quiet Soi Ruam Rudi. His fixed prices and good service make him a popular choice among expats.
☎ 0 2253 8582
✉ 28/7 Soi Ruam Rudi, Th Ploenchit
🚆 Ploenchit 🚶 fair

A sterling idea: silver setting at SV Jewellery

All that Glitters

Ah, the gem scam. We all know of someone who's been duped but, still, it's so easy to be lulled into a false sense of security in the Land of Smiles. Let the warning bells ring when a friendly local approaches you and, after some chatter, casually asks you along to their friend's gem (and/or tailoring) shop or a one-day-only sale. The gem scam usually ends with you being talked into buying low-grade gems and posting them home, where you'll find out they're worth very little. Just remember that your average Thai doesn't just start talking to strange foreigners and a deal too good to be true almost certainly is.

CLOTHING

Fly Now (4, F2) Designer Chamnan Phakdeesuk has flown his flowing, feminine designs all the way to London and back (having opened at London Fashion Week twice) and still effortlessly lands on the daily runways of Bangkok's fashion elite.
☎ 0 2656 1359 ✉ 2nd fl, Gaysorn Plaza, cnr Th Ploenchit & Th Ratchadamri ⏰ 10am-9pm ⓡ Chitlom ♿ good

Greyhound (5, D2) Greyhound makes sleek streetwear – basics with an edge – for urbanites. Like many fashion houses, it's expanding to become a lifestyle brand that includes its chain of minimalist Greyhound Cafes (see p73). Also in Siam Center (4, D2) and Central Chitlom (4, F2).
☎ 0 2260 7121 🖥 www.greyhound .co.th ✉ 2nd fl, the Emporium, btwn Sois 22 & 24, Th Sukhumvit ⏰ 10.30am-10pm

ⓡ **Phrom Phong** ♿ **good**

Jaspal (4, D2) With a finger on the pulse of Western trends and a constant eye on the international fash mags, Jaspal is a home-grown, high-street label for guys and girls. Also at the Emporium (5, D2) and Central World Plaza (4, F2).
☎ 0 2658 1000-19 ✉ Siam Discovery Center, cnr Th Phayathai & Th Phra Ram I ⏰ 10am-9pm ⓡ Siam Square ♿ good

Mae Fah Luang (4, D2) Knobby cotton suits with petal pleats and romantic lines evoke the femininity of the 1940s but in new millennium colours. It's hard to believe that such a fusion of fashion and quality has an altruistic angle. Founded by HRH the late Princess Mother, Mae Fah Luang helps villages in northern Thailand put aside opium for textile production. Also

at Suan Lum Night Bazaar (4, G5).
☎ 0 2658 0424 🖥 www.doitung.org ✉ 4th fl, Siam Discovery Center, cnr Th Phayathai & Th Phra Ram I ⏰ 10am-9pm ⓡ Siam Square 🚌 16, 21, 25, 40, 141 ♿ good

Eye-piercing: classic sequins

CLOTHING & SHOE SIZES

Women's Clothing

Aust/UK	8	10	12	14	16	18
Europe	36	38	40	42	44	46
Japan	5	7	9	11	13	15
USA	6	8	10	12	14	16

Women's Shoes

Aust/USA	5	6	7	8	9	10
Europe	35	36	37	38	39	40
France only	35	36	38	39	40	42
Japan	22	23	24	25	26	27
UK	3½	4½	5½	6½	7½	8½

Men's Clothing

Aust	92	96	100	104	108	112
Europe	46	48	50	52	54	56

	S	M	M		L	
Japan						
UK/USA	35	36	37	38	39	40

Men's Shirts (Collar Sizes)

Aust/Japan	38	39	40	41	42	43
Europe	38	39	40	41	42	43
UK/USA	15	15½	16	16½	17	17½

Men's Shoes

Aust/UK	7	8	9	10	11	12
Europe	41	42	43	44½	46	47
Japan	26	27	27.5	28	29	30
USA	7½	8½	9½	10½	11½	12½

Measurements approximate only; try before you buy.

TAILORS & THAI SILK

Alta Moda (4, F2) Silk doesn't take your fancy or, ahem, suit your tailoring needs? Then drop by this shop en route to your tailor to select from slippery satins, starchy linens and soft cottons. Its huge showroom imports bolts and bolts of fabric from international design houses like YSL and Versace. Also at the Emporium (5, D2).
☎ 0 2255 9533 ⊠ 1st fl, Central World Plaza, cnr Th Phra Ram I & Th Ratchadamri ⏰ 10am-9pm 🚇 Chitlom 🛥 *khlong* taxi to Tha Pratunam ♿ good

Jim Thompson (7, B1) As you'd expect of the company that single-handedly resurrected the Thai silk industry, you get nothing but impeccable fabric here. You can buy silk by the metre (which can be tailored on site), silk scarves and neckties and accessories (tablecloths, throw pillows, napkins). The branch on the fourth floor of the Emporium (5, D2) carries more cutting-edge designs.
☎ 0 2632 8100 🖳 www.jimthompson .com ⊠ 9 Th Surawong ⏰ 9am-9pm 🚇 Sala Daeng ⦿ Silom ♿ fair

Lea Silk (4, G1) Dutch-born textile artist Lea Laarakker Dingjan employs village women in the famed silk-weaving province of Surin to produce the jewel-toned fabric that she uses as a canvas for her striking modern designs. A large percentage of the profits from her store is re-invested into the communities.
☎ 0 2258 2332 🖳 www.banrengkhai .com ⊠ 1st fl, Promenade Arcade, Raffles Nai Lert Park, 2/4 Th Withayu ⏰ 11am-7pm 🚇 Chitlom 🚌 62, 76 🛥 *khlong* taxi to Tha Withayu ♿ good

Miss Hong (5, A2) The highly recommended Miss Hong has been making women and children's clothes for years and is known for her attention to detail. Call to make an appointment to see her in her studio in the heart of Little Arabia. It's a good idea to take along a picture to show what look and style you're after.
☎ 0 2253 5662 ⊠ 6/25-6 Soi 3, Th Sukhumvit 🚇 Nana ♿ good

Raja's Fashions (5, A2) Raja's thrives on a top-notch reputation for men's tailoring (it seems to have besuited Bangkok's entire US expat population). Just wait for the final fitting when Raja will tell you, like every one of your predecessors, 'You came in good looking and now you're looking good'. Why change a winning formula?
☎ 0 2253 8379 ⊠ 1/6 Soi 4, Th Sumhumvit ⏰ Mon-Sat 10.30am-8pm 🚇 Nana ♿ good

Suit Yourself
Nothings fits? If you're not Thai-sized, your best bet is to get clothes made by a tailor, but don't jump into the changing room with just any needle pusher. Finding a good tailor is an involved courtship that requires sartorial savvy.
- Ask to see works in progress and inspect these for quality workmanship (double stitching, lining, extra structural details).
- Commission a few small items (shirts, pants, skirts) before returning for a high-priced suit.
- Don't go for deals offering one suit, two shirts, three ties, with an extra safari suit thrown in, for US$100 – the product will be too bad to be true.
- Bring a magazine picture to show what you want. You may fancy yourself as a George Clooney-type but they might be thinking Bill Gates.
- Insist on at least two fittings and allow at least two weeks for the final product to be completed.

ARTS & CRAFTS

Look out for celadon (green-glazed porcelain) and *benjarong* (five-colour porcelain) pieces, blue-and-white china, wickerware, hand-beaten silverware and bronzeware, woven cottons and silks, nielloware (silver inlaid with niello) and *khon* masks.

Chitlada Shop (3, F1)
This is probably as close as you'll get to the royal family, so remember to dress respectfully (women must wear long skirts and closed shoes to gain entrance). Located at the palace, this is an outlet of the nonprofit SUPPORT organisation which promotes traditional craft-making skills.
☎ 0 2282 8435 ✉ Chitlada Palace, Th Ratchawithi ☾ 10am-4.30pm 🚌 510, 18, 28 ♿ good

Maison des Arts (4, B6)
Hand-hammered, stainless steel tableware haphazardly occupies this warehouse retail shop. The bold style dates from the 15th century and staff apply no pressure to indecisive shoppers.
☎ 0 2233 6297 ✉ 1334 Th Charoen Krung ☾ Mon-Sat 11am-6pm 🚇 Saphan Taksin 🚌 75, 115, 116 ⚓ Tha Oriental ♿ limited

Nandakwang (5, C2)
There's a comforting feel about Nandakwang, from the woven drinks coasters to the embroidered stuffed animals. It will be hard to leave without fondling one of the rugged leather-bottomed satchels.
☎ 0 2258 1962 ✉ 108/3 Soi 23, Th Sukhumvit ☾ Mon-Sat 9am-5pm, Sun 10am-5pm 🚇 Nana ♿ good

Narai Phand (4, F2) As a not-for-profit enterprise for distributing villagers' handicrafts, Narai Phand has its heart in the right place, although it feels a bit like a souvenir factory.
☎ 0 2252 4670 ✉ 127 Th Ratchadamri ☾ 10am-9pm 🚇 Chitlom ⚓ *khlong* taxi to Tha Pratunam ♿ limited

Rasi Sayam (5, B1) Once you tire of souvenir kitsch, head to Rasi Sayam for *objets d'art*. Based in a Thai house, it sells delicate woven wall-hangings and intricate baskets, as well as pottery and sandstone statues.
☎ 0 2258 4195 ✉ 32 Soi 23, Th Sukhumvit ☾ Mon-Sat 9am-5.30pm 🚇 Asoke ♿ fair

Silom Village Trade Centre (4, C5) It's blissfully easy to wander around this cluster of shops. Some vendors sell the ubiquitous touristy fare while the antique shops have carved teak wall decorations to turn your house into a traditional Thai home.
✉ 286 Th Silom Chong Nonsi ☾ 10am-9pm 🚌 502, 504, 505, 15 ♿ good

Suan Lum Night Bazaar (4, G5) Suan Lum is a huge government-backed night market selling modern Thai souvenirs and handicrafts that rank a notch above the street-stall varieties. Bargaining is almost nonexistent.
✉ cnr Th Withayu & Th Phra Ram IV ☾ 6pm-midnight 🚌 13, 17, 76, 106 🚇 Lumphini ♿ good

Takee Taakon (6, B1)
This shop has a beautiful selection of hand-weaving from the silk-producing regions, especially from northern Thailand. If you're convinced mum isn't going to dig a 'McShit' T-shirt, you'll also find a small assortment of classy handicraft souvenirs.
☎ 0 2629 1473 ✉ 118 Th Phra Athit, Banglamphu ☾ Mon-Sat 10am-9pm 🚌 15, 53 ⚓ Tha Phra Athit (Banglamphu) ♿ fair

Thai Home Industries (3, F9) You can wander at will around this enormous traditional Thai building overflowing with boxes. The staff leave you to your own devices to poke around the bronzeware, silverware (especially cutlery) and basketry. Keep an eye out for the great temple bells.
☎ 0 2234 1736 ✉ 35 Soi Oriental, Th Charoen Krung ☾ 10am-8pm 🚌 75, 115, 116 ⚓ Tha Oriental ♿ good

ANTIQUES & DÉCOR

L'Arcadia (5, C2) The buyer at l'Arcadia has a sharp eye for collectibles from Burma, Cambodia and Thailand, including Sukhothai cabinets, cute red-lacquer containers, Khmer-style sandstone figures and carved, wooden temple decorations. If you simply can't resist that Burmese lounge chair, the shop can arrange to have it shipped home.
☎ 0 2259 9595
✉ 12/2 Soi 23, Th Sukhumvit ☼ 9am-10pm
🚇 Asoke ♿ fair

Nagi Arts (4, G2) Once a hobbit hole of a shop, Nagi has moved to a larger facility directly across the street from Raffles Nai Lert Park Hotel. But the collection is just as eclectic as before with antique silks and jewellery from throughout Thailand and Cambodia alongside quirky Siamese adventure books, old maps and lithographs from Asian journals.
☎ 0 2253 2826
✉ 27/4 Th Withayu
☼ Mon-Sun 10am-7pm
🚇 Chitlom 🚌 62, 76
⛵ khlong taxi to Tha Withayu ♿ good

Old Maps & Prints (3, E8) You could poke around in this shop for hours, flipping through the maps of Siam and Indochina, laughing at early explorers' quaint drawings of 'the natives' and sighing with delight at the exquisite framed prints.
☎ 0 2237 0077/8
🖥 www.classicmaps.com ✉ 4th fl, River City,

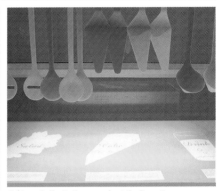
Designer ladles in Propaganda at the Emporium

Th Yotha ☼ 11am-7pm 🚌 75, 93 🚢 Tha Si Phraya ♿ good

Propaganda (5, D2) If Propaganda is truly trying to live up to its name, then count us as officially indoctrinated. It's hard to resist the charms of this fun, stark-white shop with all sorts of functional design pieces created by Thai designers, like Chaiyut Plypetch's lamps featuring the anatomically cartoonish Mr P. Another branch in Siam Discovery Center (4, D2).
☎ 0 2664 8574
✉ 4th fl, the Emporium, btwn Sois 22 & 24, Th Sukhumvit

☼ 10.30am-10pm Mon-Fri, 10am-10pm Sat & Sun 🚇 Phrom Phong ♿ good

Triphum (4, F2) Once the design makeover television shows go head over heels for Asiana instead of Victoriana, you'll be glad you mined this treasure-trove store. Fine reproductions of mother-of-pearl inlaid cabinets and lacquerware scripture chests are just the antidote to a world mad for doilies.
☎ 0 2656 1795 ✉ 3rd fl, Gaysorn Plaza, cnr Th Ploenchit & Th Ratchadamri ☼ 10am-9pm
🚇 Chitlom ♿ good

Love Hurts
Be careful before you start falling in love with images or statues of Buddha and other deities. For any image that isn't an amulet (intended for religious purposes), you'll need a licence from the Department of Fine Arts and a permit from the Ministry of Commerce. If you want to take an antique home, you need to apply for a licence from Fine Arts. Contact the National Museum on ☎ 0 2226 1661 for more information.

MUSIC & BOOKS

Asia Books (5, B2) You can't beat Asia Books for its sheer breadth of English-language titles and its huge selection of books on Asia. Also at Siam Discovery Center (4, D2), the Emporium (5, D2), Landmark Bangkok (5, A2), Peninsula Plaza (4, F2), Thaniya Plaza (7, B2) and Central World Plaza (4, F2).
☎ 0 2252 7277
✉ 221 Th Sukhumvit at Soi 15 🕑 9am-9pm
🚇 Asoke 🔕 fair

Bookazine (4, E2) For a magazine fix, head to Bookazine, which imports an excellent range of glossies from around the world in many languages, as well as major newspapers. Its English-language book selection isn't bad and it sells foreign-language literature. Also at CP Tower (7, B2) and Silom Complex (7, C2).
☎ 0 2255 3778
✉ 286 Siam Sq
🕑 10am-10pm
🚇 Siam Square 🔕 fair

New DJ Siam (4, E2) In the heart of teen-landia, this tiny store feeds the kiddies with the hottest overseas alt-options as well as all the Thai-bred indie groups.
☎ 0 22251 2513
✉ 292/16 Siam Square, Soi 4 🕑 10am-5pm
🚇 Siam Square 🔕 fair

Pirated CD Stalls (6, B3) The music industry shut down Napster but they haven't put a dent in Bangkok's pirated CD market.

Bangkok in Print

Unfortunately, the two genres dominating most recent English-language fiction on Bangkok are the middle-aged or college-kid sex-capade. Some better reads are:
- *Hello My Big Big Honey!: Love Letters to Bangkok Bar Girls and Their Revealing Interviews,* edited by Dave Walker & Richard S Ehrlich
- *Jasmine Nights,* a coming-of-age novel by SP Somtow
- *Bangkok,* a historical memoir by the dean of expats, William Warren
- *Bangkok 8* by John Burdett, a 'hard-boiled' crime thriller; the protagonist is a Thai police officer

Bookworm got the travel bug? Read up at Asia Books in Sukhumvit

If you choose to flout international copyright laws, ask around for which vendor has the best quality bootlegs and do a test run before stacking up on 100B CDs.
✉ stalls dot Th Khao San & Soi Rambutri ☽ 11am-11pm 🚌 506, 53
⚓ Tha Phra Athit (Banglamphu) ♿ good

Rim Khob Fah Bookstore (3, C4) For the pseudo nerds, this bookstore has lots of glossy books on Thai arts and culture. Without committing loads of baht, you can sample an array of skinny scholarly publications from the Fine Arts Department on such topics as *What is a Buddha Image?*
☎ 0 2622 3510
✉ 78/1 Th Ratchadamnoen, Democracy Monument ☽ 8.30am-7pm
🚌 511, 512 ⚓ *khlong taxi to Tha Phan Fah* ♿ fair

Shaman Books (6, B3) As you would expect, well-thumbed Jack Kerouac paperbacks are in abundance. There's also an exciting selection of Asian travel literature and non-fiction (slim on guidebooks, though). Shaman is not the cheapest second-hand bookshop around but it's certainly one of the best organised (with a computer catalogue). It also buys used books.
☎ 0 2629 0418 ✉ 71 Th Khao San ☽ 8am-11pm
🚌 506, 53 ⚓ Tha Phra Athit (Banglamphu)
♿ fair

Currying Flavour

To transport home a sensory scrapbook of Thailand, stop by Bangkok's many food stores that stock treats for homesick Thai expats and gift-giving locals. A variety of coconut-based sweets and dried fish are available in vacuum-sealed bags at **Champ Maboonkrong** (4, D2; ☎ 0 2970 9838; 4th floor, MBK, Th Phayathai & Th Phra Ram I; ☽ 11am-10pm; Skytrain National Stadium). Fit-to-travel curry pastes, available from **Nittaya Curry Shop** (6, C2; ☎ 0 2282 8212; 136-40 Th Chakraphong; ☽ 10am-7pm; bus No 506, 17; ferry Tha Phra Athit, Banglamphu), can reproduce all these exotic flavours in your home kitchen.

FOR CHILDREN

Big kids will be fighting for the animal-shaped kites sold at Chatuchak, Sanam Luang and Lumphini Park in kite-flying season. The tourist markets are great for kids – Banglamphu has a stall of Batman and Superman outfits and fairy costumes.

Motif & Maris (4, C5)
It's rare to find someone in the rag trade still dedicated to the old arts of embroidery and smocking, so Motif & Maris is a surprise. Every piece of children's clothing hanging in this little shop is intricate and exquisite. The handmade soft toys and nursery accessories are pretty gorgeous, too. Also at River City (2, E8).
☎ 0 2635 9111
✉ 296/7 Th Silom
🕙 10am-10pm
🚌 502, 504, 505 ♿ fair

**Pet Farm Workshop
(5, D2)** If you've got loads of patience, your little one should have a ball at this make-your-own-stuffed-toy shop. First the children pick the toy's face and coat, then they choose its stuffing and voice. From there it's off to the hairdresser to fluff up the coat before a quick trip to the stylist for an outfit. Swing past the registrar for the birth certificate and then the toy's all theirs.
☎ 0 2664 8000 ✉ 3rd fl, Jamboree, the Emporium, btwn Sois 22 & 24, Th

Sukhumvit 🕙 Mon-Fri 10.30am-10pm, Sat & Sun 10am-10pm 🚉 Phrom Phong ♿ good

Plan Creations (4, D6)
If Lego people went organic, you'd have a pretty close approximation of Plan Creations' imaginative wooden toys, made from Thai rubber. To fill that

lingering Christmas list, there are blocks, pull-along alligators and play sets (like Noah's Ark and all the critters) targeted at children aged three to ten.
☎ 0 2236 9410
🖥 www.plantoys.com
✉ 114/1 Soi 10, Th Sathon 🕙 Mon-Fri 10am-6pm, Sat 10am-4pm
🚉 Chong Nonsi ♿ fair

Flight of fancy: kites for sale at Sanam Luang

Taxing Stuff Indeed
If you can make sense of the tangled web of guidelines, you can claim back some of the VAT you've paid. To qualify, you must have spent at least 5000B on the goods, which must be bought at participating stores (a minimum 2000B spent per visit), where you have to show your passport and complete the appropriate forms. You also must have been in Thailand for fewer than 180 days in a calendar year, be leaving the country by plane and apply at the airport departure hall.

Eating

It's a rare moment when Bangkok residents aren't eating, planning their next meal or swapping restaurant notes. Food is everywhere, from chic eateries to street-side stalls. The city's best restaurants are glorified family kitchens where dressing to impress means wiping down the laminate tables. Almost every corner boasts a small army of street vendors ranging from specialty carts to the venerable name-that-dish maestros. Of the foreign-born meals, Italian translates well into Bangkok's steamy climate, but every European cuisine has an outpost for homesick expats. Districts like Little Arabia, Little India and Chinatown are dynamic areas with authentic restaurants for the local communities.

Eating, Thai-style

Eating is a social occasion to be shared with as many people as possible. The head of the table typically orders a combination of dishes, which arrive in no particular order since they will be eaten family style. Foreigners who insist on ordering individually (and not sharing) are frequently frustrated by the kitchen's poor timing.

The famous curries *(kaeng)* and soups (such as *tôm yam kûng*) are served in communal bowls from which you ladle the contents into an individual bowl and then spoon the edible bits on to rice. Not everything is edible; if it is hard to chew, then you've discovered the Thai version of bay leaves.

Thais eat with a spoon and a fork, using the fork to push food onto the spoon. To them, putting a fork in the mouth is the height of bad manners. It's OK to use your hands when eating sticky rice; roll the rice into a ball and eat it with your right hand. You'll only be offered chopsticks with noodle soups *(kǔaytǐaw)* or certain Chinese meals.

Drinks

Beer is a tasty complement to Thai food and can cut through the famous chilli sting. Pilsners, like Singha (pronounced sing), Heineken, Beer Chang and Kloster are all common choices. An ingenious but provincial custom is

<table>
<tr><td colspan="2">Meal Costs</td></tr>
<tr><td colspan="2">The pricing symbols used in this chapter indicate the cost of a two-course meal for one person, including all taxes and charges, and excluding drinks.</td></tr>
<tr><td>$</td><td>under 99B</td></tr>
<tr><td>$$</td><td>100–349B</td></tr>
<tr><td>$$$</td><td>350–599B</td></tr>
<tr><td>$$$$</td><td>over 600B</td></tr>
</table>

Dish it: share and share alike

the addition of ice cubes to glasses of beer in order to keep the beverage cool. For the sophisticates, though, wine is the only respectable tableside date, even though it tends to skunk in Bangkok's hellish climate. Wine is best ordered from places that have dedicated cellars and are able to ensure temperature control.

THAI FOOD

Thai cuisine can be both delicate and explosive, sophisticated and simple. But even though it swings between such extremes, its secret ingredient is balance. To understand this, just look at a typical Thai dinner table – laden with curry, salad, stir-fry, soup, vegetables and fish dishes – a broad range of flavours. Diners add condiments to each of these dishes to change the balance between the four key flavours – chilli to adjust the heat, fish sauce for the saltiness, vinegar with chilli for the sourness and sugar for the sweetness. The only dish not to be tinkered with is the rice *(khâo)*, which is so crucial to Thai culture that *kin khâo* (literally 'to eat rice') is the phrase for eating. The second-most revered staple is the humble noodle.

Herbs, Spices & Chillies

Thai food would be nothing without the punch of its herbs and spices, not to mention the king hit of chilli. Thais have an emotional attachment to their chillies and you, too, may well get a bit teary after a few potent bird's eye chillies lurking in spicy salads. Other key flavours come from coriander, basil (three varieties), lemon grass, ginger, galangal, garlic and shallots.

Street Food

The classic Bangkok eating experience is sitting on a plastic stool by the side of a traffic-choked road and eating a bowl of noodles or a simple rice dish cooked in front of you. Locals, both rich and poor, will travel any distance to their favourite stall – it's not rare to see Mercedes parked alongside motorbikes.

Some stalls are so famous that articles are written about them in both Thai and English newspapers (look for the clippings proudly displayed beside the nightly inventory). You'll need a little Thai to order, as English can be limited. The book *Thai Hawker Food* (available at most Bangkok bookstores) is also a good start for getting your bearings.

Here are a few street-food recommendations and tips on spotting their purveyors:
- *sôm-tam* (green papaya salad) – look for a large wooden mortar and order it with *khâo nǐaw* (sticky rice)
- *phàt thai* (thin rice noodles with tofu, vegetables, egg and peanuts) – any vendor with a wok can make this, but quality varies
- *kǔaytǐaw phàt khîi mao* (literally 'shit-drunk noodles'; wide rice noodles combined with meat, vegetables, chilli and Thai basil) – another wok wonder
- *khâo phàt* (stir-fried rice) – also available from wok vendors
- *khâo man kài* (chicken and rice) – look for carcasses of boiled chicken in the display case

BANGLAMPHU & KO RATANAKOSIN

The old quarter of Bangkok, dominated by backpackers, civil servants and artists, has a tasty assortment of unpretentious Thai restaurants.

Arawy (3, C4) $
Thai Vegetarian
Blink and you'll miss this vegetarian eatery, not only because it's small and inconspicuous, but also because its roman-script sign says 'Alloy'. Arawy was one of the city's first vegetarian restaurants and it's still going strong, serving pre-made dishes like pumpkin stir-fry and green curry.
✉ 152 Th Din So
☽ 7am-7pm 🚌 511, 42
🚣 *khlong* taxi to Tha Phan Fah ♿ good
🧑 Ⓥ

Baan Phanfah Restaurant (2, D4) $$
Thai Restaurant-Bar-Gallery
Spot-on Thai cuisine is mastered within the gracious surroundings of a converted Sino-Portuguese mansion on Khlong Banglamphu. Choose between the outdoor courtyard serenaded by moody lounge music or inside where crisp white walls are adorned with changing modern art exhibitions. In either perch, go for the daring *sôm-tam* (green papaya salad).
☎ 0 2281 6237

🖥 www.baanphan fah.com ✉ 591 Th Phra Sumen ☽ 11am-midnight 🚌 511, 512
🚣 *khlong* taxi to Tha Phan Fah ♿ fair

Coffee & More (6, B2) $
Café
Homes-away-from-home can be dangerous. Once you've plunged into a big lounge chair and a game of chess, with great coffee to sustain you, it's hard to pull yourself out. At night the chill-out music gets louder and the lounge lizards become lounge lushes.
☎ 0 2280 7878
✉ 102/1 Th Phra Athit ☽ 11am-10pm Mon-Fri, 11am-11pm Sat & Sun
🚌 15, 53
🚣 *khlong* taxi to Tha Phra Athit (Banglamphu) ♿ fair Ⓥ

Hemlock (6, A2) $$
Thai Restaurant-Bar
You've met this restaurant before — remember that cosy gem where you wooed countless dates? Hemlock is just such a creature boasting a steady cast of artsy types and an eclectic menu

that strolls through the owner's personal favourites.
☎ 0 2282 7507
✉ 56 Th Phra Athit
☽ 4pm-midnight Mon-Fri, 5pm-midnight Sat
🚌 15, 53 🚣 *khlong* taxi to Tha Phra Athit (Banglamphu)
♿ good Ⓥ

Isan restaurants (3, E3) $$
Northeastern Thai
When a boxing match is on at nearby Ratchadamnoen Stadium, these simple restaurants are run off their feet serving plates of Isan staples like *kài yâang* (grilled chicken), *sôm-tam* (green papaya salad) and *khâo nĭaw* (sticky rice). A fun pre-match tradition, the chicken is too dry to qualify as a main event.
✉ Th Ratchadamnoen Nok ☽ 11am-10pm
🚌 503, 509, 70
♿ good 🧑

Khrua Nopparat (6, B1) $
Thai
It may have a groovy factor of zilch (uncommon round these parts) but the food factor rockets off the scale. Local Thai families and workmates crowd this joint to eat plates of yummy everyday Thai dishes at little more than street prices.
☎ 0 2281 7578
✉ 136 Th Phra Athit
☽ 10.30am-9.30pm Mon-Sat 🚌 15, 53
🚣 Tha Phra Athit (Banglamphu)
♿ good 🧑 Ⓥ

Strictly Vegetarian
It's tough to be truly vegetarian at Thai restaurants. You can ask for 'no meat or seafood' but then your dish arrives with fish sauce. But you won't need to worry at strictly vegetarian places like Arawy and Tamarind Café (p74) or Indian restaurants like Chennai Kitchen (p77) or Dosa King (p72). Don't miss Chinatown during its annual Vegetarian Festival.

Krisa Coffee Shop (3, B4) $
Thai
Krisa Coffee Shop is a nifty pit stop during a hot trek around the temples and palaces of Ratanakosin – it's air-conditioned and serves up cheap and cheerful one-plate meals, like *kŭaytĭaw phàt khĭi mao* (wide rice noodles with holy basil and chilli), to see you through the expedition.
☎ 0 2225 2680 ✉ Th Na Phra Lan ⏲ 10am-8pm 🚌 506, 512 🚢 Tha Chang ♿ fair ⚹

Ricky's Coffee Shop (6, A2) $$
Café
Ricky's is a beautiful café, decorated like an old Chinese shopfront and decked out with old fans and cigarette poster-girl prints. And it knows its market so well, serving the best baguette sandwiches in Banglamphu. Pity about the unreliable service and bland Thai food.
☎ 0 2846 3011 ✉ 22 Th Phra Athit ⏲ 8am-midnight 🚌 15, 53 🚢 Tha Phra Athit (Banglamphu) ♿ fair Ⓥ

Roti Mataba (6, B1) $
Muslim
Don't visit Banglamphu without stopping by Roti Mataba. Even if you're not hungry, you can watch the rhythms of the roti-makers as they slap and flip the Indian-style bread on the hotplate. But it's hard to resist fresh crunchy roti dipped in chicken korma or stuffed with vegetables.
☎ 0 2282 2119 ✉ 136 Th Phra Athit ⏲ 7am-8pm Tue-Sun

Less rice, more slice: Banglamphu's sandwich guru

🚌 15, 53 🚢 Tha Phra Athit (Banglamphu) ♿ fair ⚹

Shoshana (6, B2) $
Israeli
Down an alley beside the petrol station on Th Chakraphong, Shoshana's is a favourite of cuisine-cruising travellers. The falafel-and-hummus plates are suitable gut bombs, but don't overlook the tasty *baba ghanoush* and *hazilim*.
✉ 86 Th Chakraphong ⏲ 11am-11pm 🚌 506, 53 🚢 Tha Phra Athit (Banglamphu) ♿ fair ⚹ Ⓥ

Thip Samai (3, D5) $
Thai
Phàt thai, the country's most common street food, still retains its venerable footpath setting but has been elevated, flavourwise, to notoriety. Wrapped in a delicate egg crepe, the special noodles are spiked with prime shrimp and achieve the perfect texture. It must be good if Thais are willing to pay 60B a plate.
☎ 0 2221 6280 ✉ 313 Th Boriphat ⏲ 5.30pm-2am 🚌 511, 512 🚢 *khlong* taxi to Tha Phan Fah ♿ good ⚹

Ton Pho (6, A2) $$
Thai
On a steamy day, try to catch a breeze at this open-air riverside restaurant, just behind Tha Phra Athit (Banglamphu). Ceiling fans rotate relentlessly overhead, as waiters scurry across the wooden floorboards (with big gaps revealing the river beneath) with excellent soups, salads and seafood.
☎ 0 2280 0452 ✉ Th Phra Athit, beside Tha Phra Athit (Banglamphu) ⏲ 11am-10pm 🚌 15, 53 🚢 Tha Phra Athit (Banglamphu) ♿ good ⚹ Ⓥ

Crickets to Go
Silly you – the average garden pest is really a tasty treat. After the rainy season, vendors appear throughout town (try Th Khao San) with conical heaps of stir-fried bugs (crickets, red ants and water beetles). Pull off the legs and pop the bugger in your mouth, where initial revulsion will turn into potato-chip addiction.

CHINATOWN & PHAHURAT

When you say 'Chinatown', Bangkokians reflexively start slurping noodles, but other Chinese victuals are just as mouth-watering. The neighbouring district of Phahurat is the city's Little India with hearty curries and deep-fried samosas.

Hong Kong Dim Sum (3, E6) $
Chinese
Amid the bustle of Chinatown's most fascinating laneway is this haven of comfort snacks – warm, fluffy, barbecued pork buns and buttery, crumbling custard tarts.
✉ 136/5 Trok Itsaranuphap near cnr of Th Charoen Krung
🕙 10am-8pm 🚌 501, 507, 73, 53 🚊 Tha Ratchawong ♿ fair 👤

Hong Kong Noodles (3, E6) $
Chinese
Next door to Hong Kong Dim Sum, this crowded noodle shop delivers aromatic bowls of roasted duck noodles (*kŭaytǐaw pèt yâang*) with slippery wontons in a restorative broth.
✉ 136/4 Trok Itsaranuphap near cnr of Th Charoen Krung
🕙 10am-8pm 🚌 501, 507, 73, 53 🚊 Tha Ratchawong ♿ fair 👤

Old Siam Plaza Food Centre (3, C6) $
Thai Sweets
Beans, rice, tapioca, corn: Thais can turn seemingly savoury ingredients into extraordinarily sweet desserts. Peruse these transformations: *lûuk chúp* (miniature fruits made of beans) and *khanŏm bêuang* (taco-shaped pancakes filled with shredded coconut and golden threads of sweetened egg yolks).
✉ ground fl, Old Siam Plaza, cnr Th Phahurat & Th Triphet 🕙 10am-5pm 🚌 507, 53 🚊 Tha Saphan Phut ♿ fair 👤

Pet Tun Jao Tha (3, E8) $
Chinese
As the name 'Harbour Department Stewed Duck' suggests, big birds are the order of the day here. You don't have to just eat the special, steamed duck and goose with rice noodles; but you'd be silly not to. This restaurant is at the far eastern edge of Chinatown, near River City.
☎ 0 2233 2541
✉ 945 Soi Charoen Phanit, Talat Noi
🕙 11am-8pm 🚌 35, 36, 75 🚊 Tha Si Phraya ♿ fair 👤

Royal India (3, C6) $$
North Indian
You are unsure as you go down the dark laneway and open an unmarked door.

A whole world of food: Old Siam Plaza Food Centre

Going it Alone

As a rule, Thais don't eat by themselves – after all, it would limit the number of dishes they can order. You might feel a bit uncomfortable at an upmarket restaurant by yourself, but you will fit right in at noodle shops, curry-rice places and night markets, which dish up one-plate meals.

When you eat in the street, you're never alone

Inside, tables of men are deep in discussion while a voluptuously moustachioed Indian man flogs golf clubs on cable TV. You soon discover that the food is incredible and the dhal indescribably delicious. Mission accomplished.

☎ 0 2221 6565
✉ 392/1 Th Chakraphet
☽ 10am-10pm 🚌 507, 73 ⚓ Tha Saphan Phut
♿ fair 🚻 Ⓥ

Shangarila (3, D6) $$$
Cantonese
Got a Peking duck craving? Haven't had a grand, slap-up Cantonese meal for a while? Don't go past Shangarila, one of Chinatown's most respected restaurants. Chinese families come to spin the lazy Susan during the restaurant's famed dim sum lunches.

☎ 0 2235 7493
✉ 206 Th Yaowarat
☽ 11am-10pm 🚌 507, 53, 73 ⚓ Tha Ratchawong
♿ fair 🚻 Ⓥ

Th Phadungdao Seafood Stalls (3, E6) $$
Chinese Seafood
After the sun goes down in the evening, this street sprouts outdoor barbecues, iced seafood trays and footpath seating. People serving food dash every which way, cars plough through narrow street openings, and before you know it you're tearing into a plate of grilled prawns like a starved alley cat. Blaring Chinese pop music and limbless beggars will make your visit an extra-surreal experience.

✉ Th Phadungdao off Th Yaowarat ☽ 6-10pm
🚌 507, 53, 73
⚓ Tha Ratchawong
♿ good 🚻

SUKHUMVIT

If you chose wisely, you can eat fabulously along this leggy street. A veritable UN of food caters to compatriots and curious Thais, with diplomatic success.

Atlanta Coffee Shop (5, A3) $
Thai
We could rave until the water buffalo come home. Not only is this the ultimate in impeccably-preserved retro coffee shops but it also takes its vegetarian Thai food seriously. Don't miss the stir-fried morning glory or the breakfasts.
☎ 0 2252 6069
✉ 78 Soi 2, Th Sukhumvit
🕓 6am-11pm
🚇 Ploenchit
♿ good 🚻 Ⓥ

Bei Otto (5, C2) $$$
German
Proudly German right down to its sausage placemats, Bei Otto is where misty-eyed expats come for roasted pig's knuckle (actually, everyone comes for that), proper bread and a frothy stein of wheat beer.
☎ 0 2262 0892
✉ 1 Soi 20, Th Sukhumvit
🕓 9am-1am
🚇 Asoke or Phrom Phong
♿ good 🚻

Cabbages & Condoms (5, B3) $$
Thai
It isn't the best Thai food in town, but it is the best cause around. Cabbages & Condoms is affiliated with the Population & Community Development Association (PDA), a sex-education/AIDS-prevention organisation credited for Thailand's speedy reaction to the AIDS crisis. In addition to meal names that would make an adolescent chuckle, diners get packaged condoms in lieu of after-dinner mints.
☎ 0 2229 4611
✉ Soi 12, Th Sukhumvit
🕓 11am-10pm
🚇 Asoke ♿ good
🚻 Ⓥ

Crepes & Co (5, B3) $$
French-Moroccan
It might sound like a sub-urban pancake franchise but Crepes & Co is an original. Delicate, platter-sized crepes stuffed with smoky bacon and woodsy mushrooms as well as thick coffee will soothe your Asian exile. Kids' menu available.
☎ 0 2653 3990
✉ 18/1 Soi 12, Th Sukhumvit 🕓 9am-midnight 🚇 Asoke
♿ fair 🚻 Ⓥ

Dosa King (5, B2) $
Indian-Vegetarian
You don't have to get all 'dhal-ed' up to dine on tasty Indian food. (Although a spiffy look would put you in league with the sari-wrapped mothers and clubbing teenagers.) Divine renditions of the Punjabi speciality, *dosa* (a thin, stuffed crepe), adorn the

Hotel Restaurants? No Worries!

Bangkok used to be ruled by hotel restaurants, which have since evolved into collection pieces, partly for pleasure but mainly for show. The hotels' most breath-taking experiences, though, are the famous stomach-popping buffets (lunch, dinner and Sunday brunch) where decadence dominates. You can hardly go wrong with any top-end hotel, but here are a few standouts:

For Sunday brunch, try the riverside setting at the **Royal Orchid Sheraton** (3, E8; ☎ 0 2266 0123, Soi Captain Bush/Soi 30, Th Charoen Krung; 750/375B), which also has kids' activities. Or sample the buffet at the **Four Seasons** (4, F2; ☎ 0 2251 6127, Four Seasons Hotel, Th Ratchadamri; 1250/625B), catered for by its well-regarded in-house restaurants. **Youzen Restaurant** (5, B2; ☎ 0 2262 1234; Windsor Suites Hotel, Soi 20, Th Sukhumvit; 300B) has a killer Japanese lunch buffet for all your raw cravings. And don't miss the chocolate or the Sunday brunch at the **Colonnade** (p77).

tables like ancient parchment scrolls.

☎ 0 2651 1651
✉ 265/1 Soi 19, Th Sukhumvit
🕐 11am-11pm 🚇 Asoke
♿ fair 👶 Ⓥ

Greyhound Cafe (5, D2) $$
International

Don't be fooled by the flimsy fashionista types picking at their pasta and the minimalism *du jour* of the design. The Greyhound Cafe is undoubtedly a very cool place to be seen but the food (Thai and fusion café favourites) is fantastic. Also at Central Chitlom (4, F2).

☎ 0 2664 8663
✉ 2nd fl, the Emporium, btwn Sois 22 & 24, Th Sukhumvit 🕐 11am-10pm 🚇 Phrom Phong
♿ good Ⓥ

Kuppa (5, C3) $$$$
International

Kuppa is *the* hot spot of the affluent thirty-somethings (especially at weekend brunchtimes), who leave their drivers sleeping in the BMW while they tuck into braised lamb shanks with lentils and other international fusion dishes.

☎ 0 2663 0495
✉ 39 Soi 16, Th Sukhumvit 🕐 10.30am-10.30pm
🚇 Asoke ♿ good Ⓥ

La Piola (5, A1) $$$$
Italian

Take a seat in this intimate basement eatery as an honoured guest of Pietro and his family. Mama is in the kitchen preparing a set menu of three courses (antipasto, three pasta mains,

Spices are sublime at Le Dalat Indochine restaurant

and dessert) that could lure Martin Luther back to the flock. Meanwhile suave cousin Pino serenades the crowd with Sinatra tunes.

☎ 0 2253 8295
✉ 32 Soi 13, Th Sukhumvit 🕐 6-10pm Tue-Sat
🚇 Nana ♿ fair

Le Dalat Indochine (5, C2) $$$
Vietnamese

The exquisite Vietnamese food almost gets sidelined by the divine surroundings when you eat in this beautifully converted old house filled with potted palms and artworks. Try the house special, *naem meuang* – grilled meatballs mixed with spices and fruit on rice paper rolls, then wrapped in lettuce.

☎ 0 2661 7967
✉ 14 Soi 23, Th Sukhumvit 🕐 11am-2.30pm & 5-10pm 🚇 Asoke ♿ fair

Mrs Balbir's (5, B2) $$$
North Indian

Mrs Balbir is a one-woman entertainment machine, her empire spanning a TV show, a cooking school (p41) and

this famous eatery. Her larger-than-life personality is part of the attraction; the North Indian food is good but not outstanding.

☎ 0 2651 0498
✉ 155/18 Soi 11/1, Th Sukhumvit 🕐 noon-10.30pm Tue-Sun
🚇 Nana ♿ fair 👶 Ⓥ

Nasir al-Masri Restaurant & Shishah (5, A2) $$
Egyptian

If there was ever a place to wear your sunglasses at night, Nasir al-Masri is it. With reflective surfaces everywhere, Nasir creates an illusion of oil-money banquets involving artistically arranged sesame-freckled flatbread, creamy hummus and flawlessly fried falafels.

☎ 0 2253 5582
✉ 4/6 Soi 3/1, Th Sukhumvit 🕐 7am-4am
🚇 Nana ♿ good 👶

Pizzeria Bella Napoli (4, B2) $$
Italian

An eclectic and boisterous crowd gulps down glasses of blood-red wine and gooey, garlicky, wood-fired

Toe-tapping: catch regional food, dance and music at Vientiane Kitchen restaurant

pizzas in this Napolese outpost. Prepare to feel horribly jealous when the party next to you orders the prosciutto-bridge pizza.
☎ 0 2259 0405
✉ 3/3 Soi 31, Th Sukhumvit ⏲ 6pm-1am Mon-Fri, noon-5pm Sat & Sun ♿ Phrom Phong ♿ good ⬧ V

Ruen-Mallika (5, C3) $$$
Thai
Thais have tourists figured out: just convert an old teak house into a restaurant and the crowds will come, regardless of the food. But Ruen-Mallika improves the formula by serving exquisite dishes, like dizzyingly spicy *náam phrík* (a thick dipping sauce with vegetables and herbs) and soulful chicken wrapped in pandanus leaves. The house signature dish of deep-fried flowers is prettier looking than tasting. Approach Ruen-Mallika by heading along Soi 16, which is off Th Ratchadapisek.
☎ 0 2663 3211
✉ sub-*soi* off Soi 22, Th Sukhumvit ⏲ 11am-11pm ♿ Asoke ♿ good

Salon de L'Oriental (5, D2) $$
Café
People-watching is at a premium in the fountain-side seats, usually occupied by ladies who lunch and princesses who shop. If you don't make it to the Oriental Hotel's high tea, this is a backup option – the scones and cucumber sandwiches arrive, like they should, on a silver-tiered server.
☎ 0 2664 8186
✉ ground fl, the Emporium, btw Sois 22 & 24, Th Sukhumvit ⏲ Mon-Fri 10.30am-10pm, Sat & Sun 10am-10pm ♿ Phrom Phong ♿ good

Soi 38 Night Market (5, F2) $
Thai-Chinese
What's a night-owl to do when all the bars close up at 2am? Never fear, the good old night market is here. Chow your way to sobriety with a bowl of *kŭaytǐaw mǔu daeng* (red pork noodles) or *kŭaytǐaw lawt* (Chinese-style spring rolls).
✉ Soi 38, Th Sukhumvit ⏲ 6pm-3am ♿ Thong Lor ♿ good

Tamarind Café (5, C2) $$
International-Vegetarian
Tamarind Café creates harmonious unions out of international ingredients, without ever visiting the butcher shop. Invite deep-fried oyster mushrooms escorted by a sweet Thai dipping sauce to your table, or pucker up to a fresh fruit juice or smoothie. Leave room for the luscious chocolate *gateaux*.
☎ 0 2663 7421
✉ 27 Soi 20, Th Sukhumvit ⏲ 11am-11pm ♿ Asoke ♿ fair ⬧ V

Vientiane Kitchen (5, E2) $$
Northeastern Thai-Lao
Want to catch some local dance and music but don't want a canned performance with lousy food? This open-air barn is alive with the music of Isan and Laos and such authentic specialities as *lâap mǔu* (minced pork salad), *kài yâang* (grilled marinated chicken) and the ubiquitous sticky rice.
☎ 0 2258 6171
✉ 8 Soi 36, Th Sukhumvit ⏲ 11am-midnight ♿ Thong Lor ♿ good ⬧

SIAM SQUARE

From mall munching to causes célèbres, Siam Square and nearby Th Ploenchit, Th Ratchadamri and Th Withayu offer a full house of eating options.

Baan Khanitha & Gallery (4, G3) $$$
Thai
Although this branch is only a few years old, Baan Khanitha is one of Bangkok's classic restaurants. Why? It's got the formula down pat: outstanding food, high-class setting, challenging art gallery and impeccable service. Also at Soi 23, Th Sukhumvit (5, B1).
☎ 0 2253 4638/9
✉ 49 Soi Ruam Rudi, Th Ploenchit ⏰ 10.30am-2pm & 6-11pm
🚇 Ploenchit ♿ fair

Foodloft (4, F2) $$
International
Practically nobody could resist Foodloft's enthusiastic slogan: 'New, trendy, up-scale, international dining concept'. Wow, what a mouthful; and all under one roof? Indeed, amid industrial chic and city views is a dressed-up cafeteria serving gourmet Italian, Indian, Japanese, Chinese, Thai and Vietnamese.
☎ 0 2655 7777 ✉ 7th fl, Central Chitlom, Th Ploenchit ⏰ 10am-10pm
🚇 Chitlom ♿ good
♿ Ⓥ

Grappino Italian Restaurant (4, F1) $$$$
Italian
Grappino has got soul. Like an Italian, it takes its wining and dining experience seriously, so it makes the pasta and bread from scratch, has a cellar to die for and always has fun. It even prides itself on its extensive grappa collection – a sure sign that the heart leads the head here.
☎ 0 2653 9000
✉ Amari Watergate Hotel, 847 Th Phetchaburi ⏰ noon-2.30pm & 6-11pm 🚌 505, 511
🚤 *khlong* taxi to Tha Pratunam ♿ good

Le Lys (4, F3) $$
Thai
A natural and relaxed beauty, Le Lys is a converted house draped in a lush garden. All the curries are divine and arrive long before your empty

---

Breakfast Is Served
Thailand's interpretation of Western-style breakfast – from the guesthouse pancake to mid-century coffee shops – is an overlooked anthropology thesis topic. To mix dining with opining, check out the Atlanta Coffee Shop (p72), the Federal Hotel coffee shop (p99) or Sorn's (p76). But for fussy gourmets, who prefer the culinary over the curious, opt for Kuppa (p73) and Crepes & Co (p72).

Food Without the Fumes

Shopping centre food courts back home are examples of food abuse, but Bangkok's food courts retain the same dedication to flavours as their street-side brethren and without the noise or heat. All the shopping centres have one, but MBK (see below) and Foodloft (p75) are genre stand-outs. The process works like this: you buy food with coupons from a designated booth and can get a refund for any unspent coupons on the day of purchase.

table could prompt nervous glances towards the kitchen. Family photos clutter the unused spaces, Thai textiles hang askew, and the family's daily life goes on without interruption.
- ☎ 0 2652 2401
- ✉ 75 Sub-Soi 3, Soi Lang Suan, Th Ploenchit
- ☾ 11am-10.30pm
- ⊕ Chitlom
- ♿ fair ♨

MBK Food Hall (4, D2) $
Chinese-Thai
It's a lot like having all your favourite street food vendors in the one place. There is no need to visit the noodle woman in one street, the fruit-juice man in another and then hike to find a mango and sticky rice stall.
- ✉ 6th fl, MBK shopping centre, cnr Th Phra Ram I & Th Phayathai
- ☾ 10am-midnight
- ⊕ National Stadium
- ♿ good ♨ V

Soi Polo Fried Chicken (3, G4) $$
Your nose will lead you to what many claim is the best *kài thâwt* (fried chicken) in town; it certainly bitch-slaps KFC. Golden and

crispy on the outside with lots of fried garlic bits, even a tentative taste will excavate moist and juicy meat within. One half-order will generously feed two. To eat like a local, order sticky rice and employ the spicy dipping sauces.
- ☎ 0 2655 8489
- ✉ 137/1-2 Soi Polo, Th Withayu ☾ 7am-7pm
- ⊕ Phloenchit
- ♿ good ♨

Sorn's (4, D1) $$
Thai-International
Wearing a bougainvillea bonnet, this shambolic garden café gruffly caters to the neighbourhood's backpackers with ubiquitous Western breakfast and fruit shakes. What distinguishes Sorn's is its

menu — one of the city's best crash courses on Thai cuisine. Bring a notebook as your dining companion to cram for future street-stall exams.
- ☎ 0 2215 5163
- ✉ 36/8 Soi Kasem San 1, Th Phra Ram I, Siam Sq
- ☾ 7am-1pm & 5-10pm
- ⊕ National Stadium
- ⚓ *khlong* taxi to Tha Ratchathewi
- ♿ good ♨ V

Whole Earth (4, F3) $$
Thai-Vegetarian
Reclining on cushions upstairs, you might come to feel like you're spending a long afternoon in your New Agey auntie's lounge room, which she has decorated with souvenirs from the 'getting spiritual' tour of Asia she undertook in the 1970s. And, if you stop to think about it, the vegetarian food is a bit like that too — homey, familiar and nutritious, but not actually all that exciting. Except for the divine fruit lassis.
- ☎ 0 2252 5574
- ✉ 93/3 Soi Lang Suan
- ☾ 11.30am-2pm & 5.30-11pm
- ⊕ Chitlom ♿ good ♨ V

Lads and lassis: suck it up at the Whole Earth restaurant

SILOM

Bangkok's financial district does a lot of wining and dining, but the Thai options tend to be beautiful but vapid – a fine choice in a second marriage but disappointing for a memorable meal. More interesting are the austere Muslim and Indian restaurants camouflaged within busy residential *soi*.

Alliance Française (4, F5) $
Café

It's fun to watch a cliché in action. The clientele at this simple, popular French café live up to every Gallic stereotype you can think of – they take their food seriously, smoke furiously, gesticulate wildly and argue about politics. The food – buttery pastries, good coffee and crunchy baguettes – is predictably French, too.
☎ 0 2670 4200 ✉ 29 Th Sathon Tai 🕑 11am-2pm 🚌 17 ♿ good ⚲

Bussaracum (4, C6) $$$
Thai

Recipes once reserved for royalty are made available to all at Bussaracum (pronounced boot-sa-ra-kam). Intricate dishes made from scratch are presented so much like works of art that it (almost) breaks your heart to dig a spoon into your delicate purple dumpling flowers and dramatically carved squash overflowing with seafood.
☎ 0 2266 6312 ✉ Sethiwan Tower, 139 Soi Pan, Th Silom 🕑 11am-2pm & 5-10.30pm 🚌 502, 504 ♿ fair

Celadon (4, F5) $$$$
Thai

Celadon is an effortless fine-dining experience, conceived as two elegant pavilions perched atop serene lotus ponds with stylishly executed classics.
☎ 0 2287 0222 ✉ Sukhothai Hotel, 13/3 Th Sathon Tai 🕑 11.30am-2.30pm & 6.30-10.30pm 🚌 17 ♿ good Ⓥ

Chennai Kitchen (4, C5) $
South Indian

In Bangkok's South Asian enclave, Chennai Kitchen is a family-run spot just down the road from the rowdy Sri Mariamman temple. *Dosa*, rather than tandoori, rules the roost.
☎ 0 2238 4141 ✉ 48/6 Soi Pan, Th Silom 🕑 10am-3pm & 6-10.30pm 🚌 502, 504 ♿ fair ⚲ Ⓥ

Colonnade (4, F5) $$$$
International

Colonnade should be awarded a medal for its untiring, relentless dedication to decadence. Every day between 2.30pm and 6pm, it trots out its chocolate buffet (verging on chocolate porn). Then on Sunday, buffets have to be lined with caviar, imported cheeses and free-flowing champagne for the jazz brunch from noon.
☎ 0 2287 0222 ✉ Sukhothai Hotel, 13/3 Th Sathon Tai 🕑 6am-midnight 🚌 17 ♿ good ⚲ Ⓥ

Eat Me (7, B3) $$$
International

Eat Me is one of Bangkok's most innovative and interesting restaurants. It throws together smart fusion dishes (like soft shell crab and linguini), cutting edge artwork and smooth modern design, coming up trumps night after night. Book for a balcony table on live jazz nights (Thursday and Saturday).
☎ 0 2238 0931 ✉ 1/6 Soi Piphat 2, off Th Convent 🕑 3pm-1am 🚇 Sala Daeng

Celadon restaurant

Kozo Sushi (7, B2) $$
Japanese
If you need some purity in your diet, become a trainspotter along the sushi train tracks of this restaurant. But be prepared for some duelling chopsticks during the hugely popular 220B all-you-can-eat lunch at this venue just off the Japanese entertainment strip of Soi Thaniya.
☎ 0 2231 2132
✉ ground fl, Thaniya Plaza, Soi Thaniya, Th Silom ⏰ 11.30am-2pm & 5.30-11pm 🚇 Sala Daeng ♿ good ⚹

Mizu's Kitchen (7, B2) $$
Japanese
Warm and salty, Mizu's occupation-era fusion of Japanese and American dishes is really the perfect nightcap after a schedule of heavy drinking. Although your reflexes will probably be dulled, use the red-and-white chequered tablecloth to screen yourself from the soy-sauce-hissing hot plates.

Late-Night Eats

You'll never go hungry in Bangkok at any hour, and Thai tipplers are especially diligent about polishing off a meal as insurance against a hangover. If a bowl of late-night noodles won't suffice, head to Soi 38's night market (p74), Mizu's Kitchen or Nasir al-Masri Restaurant & Shishah (p73).

☎ 0 2233 6447
✉ 32 Soi Patpong 1, Th Silom ⏰ 11am-3am
🚇 Sala Daeng
♿ good ⚹

Sara-Jane's (4, D6) $$
Isan-Italian
A real circus at lunchtime, this restaurant (named after the American founder who married a Thai) knows its Isan food. That's why expats and Thais keep coming back for the juicy, flavoursome *yam sôm oh* (pomelo salad). The original at Sindhorn Tower (4, G3; ☎ 0 2650 9992; ground floor, 130-132 Th Withayu) isn't as adept.
☎ 0 2676 338
✉ 55/21 Narathiwat Rat-chanakarin ⏰ 11am-9pm
🚌 taxi ♿ good ⚹

Soi Pradit (Soi 20) Market (4, C5) $
Thai
Bangkok's magic is working if you start craving spontaneous street-stall meals instead of air-conditioned luxury. During the day, fruit vendors and closet-sized noodle shops line this narrow *soi* leading to Masjid Mirasuddeen mosque. Look for the duck noodle shop (identified by a, um, duck sign) or rickety tables selling zesty *khanŏm jiin* (stark white rice noodles served with curries). The woks are still sizzling at night when more sit-down stalls start to appear.
✉ Soi 20, Th Silom
⏰ 10am-10pm
🚌 502, 504 ♿ good ⚹

Somboon Seafood (4, C5) $$$
Chinese Seafood
The surroundings are nothing to write home about, but you won't be keen to go home once you have eaten a big bowl of Somboon Seafood's famous crab curry. If you don't fancy getting dinner all over the place, opt for the slightly more dainty pursuit of devouring a whole fried fish.
☎ 0 2234 3104
✉ 169/7-11 Th Surawong
⏰ 4-11.30pm 🚌 75, 93
♿ good ⚹ Ⓥ

The hand is quicker than the eye: Kozo Sushi, Silom

RIVERSIDE

By Riverside, we mean the area along Mae Nam Chao Phraya in the southwest of the old city, both on the Bangkok and Thonburi banks.

Angelini (4, A6) $$$$
Italian

Angelini manages to be simultaneously grand and relaxed. It could easily be too posh for words, what with such high prices (for excellent Italian dishes, mind you) and extravagant decor, but somehow the riverside location just brings it down to earth nicely.
☎ 0 2236 7777
✉ ground fl, Shangri-La Wing, Shangri-La Hotel, 89 Soi Wat Suan Phlu, Th Charoen Krung
🕐 11am-midnight
🚤 Saphan Taksin 🚢 Tha Oriental or Tha Sathon
♿ good

Ban Chiang (4, C6) $$
Thai

Hot chips will never again satisfy your cravings for something fried and crunchy once you've eaten the *yam plaa dùk fuu* (salad with fried grated catfish) at Ban Chiang. The other Isan specialities served in this atmospheric wooden Thai house are just as lip-smackingly good.
☎ 0 2236 7045
✉ 14 Th Si Wiang, Th Surasak 🕐 11am-2pm & 5-10.30pm
🚤 Surasak ♿ fair ♿

Harmonique (3, F9) $$
Chinese-Thai

If you have been burned by your courtship with Thai food, then let Harmonique whisper sweet nothings to your tender palate.

Ban Chiang: purveyor of fried grated catfish

Its reserved dishes are served in the courtyard of a rambling wooden house bubbling over with ambience, from the huge banyan tree draped with fairy lights to the marble-top tables.
☎ 0 2630 6763
✉ 22 Soi 34, Th Charoen Krung 🕐 Mon-Sat 11am-10pm 🚢 Tha Oriental
♿ good ♿ V

Indian Hut (3, F9) $$$
North Indian

Paneer, paneer, paneer. We can't stress it enough:

don't walk out the door of Indian Hut without tasting its delectable homemade cottage cheese, preferably in its incarnation as part of the deceptively simple tomato and onion curry. Despite the fast-food overtones in the name of the restaurant, this place is very classy and popular with business-people.
☎ 0 2237 8812
✉ 311/2-5 Th Surawong 🕐 11am-3pm & 6.30-10.30pm 🚢 Tha Oriental
♿ fair ♿ V

High Tea

High tea is such an institution in Bangkok, you'd have thought Thailand was colonised. Tea in the Oriental Hotel's Author's Lounge (3, E9) is all potted plants, cane furniture and tiered silver servers. The Four Seasons Bangkok (4, F2) offers grand surroundings and a string quartet, while the Colonnade (p77) has an indecently divine chocolate buffet. High tea goes from around 2.30pm to around 6pm.

Le Normandie (3, E9) $$$$

French

Give yourself time to prepare for Le Normandie, one of Bangkok's finest. Make sure the jacket and tie are dry-cleaned and the booking is confirmed. Discipline your stomach and get your mind ready for some big decisions: the degustation or roast lobster with handmade egg noodles and bisque sauce? Leave room for the scrumptious raspberry gratin crowned with a raspberry liqueur ice cream.

☎ 0 2236 0400
✉ Oriental Hotel, Soi Oriental, Th Charoen Krung ⏰ Mon-Sat noon-2.30pm & 7-10.30pm 🚤 Tha Oriental ♿ good

Mei Jiang (4, A6) $$$$

Cantonese

Quite intentionally, the Peninsula has sited Mei Jiang on its ground floor, a good 20 storeys away from sweeping city vistas. The aim is to make you focus on internal matters, namely the Art Deco-influenced interior design and the inside of your stomach, which will be eagerly anticipating the Peking duck and other Cantonese creations.

☎ 0 2861 2888
✉ Peninsula Hotel, 333 Th Charoen Nakhon, Thonburi ⏰ 11.30am-2.30pm & 6-10pm Mon-Sat, 11am-2.30pm & 6-10pm Sun 🚤 hotel shuttle boat from Tha Sathon ♿ fair

Tongue Thai (3, F9) $$

Thai

Maybe the name is supposed to remind us of the chef's honourable intentions to not sacrifice Thai flavours to Western palates. Anyway, your tongue will be feeling most Thai as it wraps itself around flavoursome morsels of spicy eggplant salad.

☎ 0 2630 9918/9
✉ 18-20 Soi 38, Th Charoen Krung ⏰ 11am-11pm 🚤 Tha Oriental ♿ good Ⓥ

Great Places to Do Business

To close a really important business deal, go for one of the five-star hotel restaurants like Angelini, Grappino or Le Normandie. But if you're after a less flashy and more low-key place to wine and dine clients, you could try Tamarind Café (p74) or Kuppa (p73).

GREAT VIEWS

Restaurants where you won't be able to keep your eyes from wandering include riverside Ton Pho (p69), Kaloang Home Kitchen (p82), Angelini, Foodloft (p75), with city views, and Celadon (p77) where you gaze out onto lotus ponds.

Rang Mahal (5, C2) $$$
South Indian
Baby, it's cold inside. There are grand white columns, luxurious furnishings and the chill of Arctic air-conditioning. But get stuck into the curries, considered Bangkok's best, and you'll be warm again. Go for the Sunday brunch or at night when the city lights look magical from up here.
☎ 0 2261 7100
✉ 19 Soi 18, Th Sukhum-vit ⏱ 11.30am-2.30pm & 6.30-10pm Mon-Sat, 11am-3pm Sun 🚇 Asoke
♿ good ♨ Ⓥ

Absorb the Arctic chill of Rang Mahal restaurant

Sirocco (4, B6) $$$$
Mediterranean
Of all the restaurant starlets, Sirocco has the whole city abuzz, thanks to its altitude, amid the Silom skyscrapers, and to the elevating effects that a fine view and fine prices have on wooing couples. Grilled Australian tenderloin and the dessert buffet stand out amid an otherwise mediocre melange.
☎ 0 2624 9554
✉ The Dome at State Tower, 63rd fl, cnr Th Silom & Th Charoen Krung
🚌 502, 504 ⛴ Tha Oriental ♿ fair

Soup, salad and seafood at Ton Pho restaurant (p69), Banglamphu

WORTH A TRIP

Kaloang Home Kitchen (3, C1) $$
Seafood

Rough and rustic, Kaloang Home Kitchen provides you with excellent seafood dishes – such as deep-fried snakehead – in a quiet position by the river and a royal boat flotilla. Follow Th Sri Ayuthaya right to its western end.

☎ 0 2281 9228
✉ 2 Th Sri Ayuthaya, Dusit
🕐 11am-11pm 🚌 506, 53, 30 🛥 Tha Thewet
♿ good 🚼

Horng Ahaan 55 (5, F2) $$
Thai-Chinese

The metro magazines will try to steer you to the latest 'white-linen' hotties, but Bangkok's real culinary beefcakes are these naked little store fronts, like Horng Ahaan 55. Too busy whipping up such crowd pleasers as saffron-spiked *poo phàt phǒng ka-rii* (crab curry), Horng Ahaan 55 opted for the skimpy décor of a gaudy Chinese shrine and a row of revered monk pictures.

☎ 0 2391 2021
✉ 1087-1091 Th Sukhumvit 🕐 6-11pm
🚇 Thong Lor
♿ good 🚼 Ⓥ

Pickle Factory (2, B4) $$
International

Just a few tables too many to be a cosy dinner party, this converted modern house rolls out homemade pizzas to a practised crowd of lay-abouts. East-meets-West pizzas defy conventional wisdom with such shocking combos as *khǐi mao* (wing beans and holy basil) and pizza vodka (yup, those are peas). Take a taxi to avoid a long, lonely walk.

☎ 0 2246 3036
✉ 55 Soi 21, Th Ratcha-withi, Victory Monument
🕐 5.30-11.30pm
🚇 Victory Monument
♿ good 🚼 Ⓥ

Victory Point (2, B4) $
Thai

Feeling like you've left your home country only to find too much of home so far away? It is time to sample a bit of the provinces within the city limits. To the right of Victory Monument is an outdoor beer garden packed with students and romancing couples watching the on-stage renditions of Thai and Western pop tunes. The menu covers all the basics, and everything is fresh, spicy and completely Thai.

✉ Victory Monument, Th Phayathai & Th Ratchawithi
🕐 6am-10pm
🚇 Victory Monument
♿ good 🚼 Ⓥ

Hold me in your tentacles... Anyone for squid?

Entertainment

Bangkok was truly the city that never slept – until the government's crackdown that, for the first time, enforced 2am closing times. Sex shows (are supposed to) have been cleaned up, clubbers are subjected to random drug tests and bouncers adamantly check for identification to prove patrons are 20 or older. This new social conservatism has taken a swipe at the city's notorious 'anything goes' attitude – midget-on-a-motorbike sex shows or drinking beer while sitting on a plastic milk-crate in a flooded *soi* at 4am.

Sànùk, or fun, is still enthusiastically pursued, albeit in a shortened time-frame. Consummate night owls, Bangkokians don't hit the clubs until midnight, then shake it for two hours and flood the night markets till the wee hours. Tourists, with no other obligations, are more dedicated to the cause of the early-bird bar special. The new social order has given the crafty entrepreneur all sorts of loopholes – beer is still sold at certain night markets or surreptitiously out of coolers once the bars close. Cocktails served at restaurants are grandfathered past the official curfew, but this may all change.

During the sanctioned hours, the Silom area is best known for Patpong's go-go bars (7, B2) but savvy barflies head to Soi 4 (7, B2), a dead-end strip crammed with lady-boys, gays and straights, or Soi 2 (7, C2), another gay scene with mixed dance clubs.

In Banglamphu, head for vibrant Th Phra Athit (p86), lined with little bars-cum-restaurants that are crowded with Thai students and artists, or Th Khao San (p86), the mama-san of partying.

If you value your beauty sleep and your liver, there's plenty to keep you amused once the sun goes down – traditional dance or theatre shows, a *muay thai* boxing match, or world-class jazz in an all-too-cosy bar.

Hands in the air: New Year Songkhran Festival (p84)

SPECIAL EVENTS

There's always something going on in Bangkok – check the TAT website (www .tourismthailand.org) or the Bangkok Tourist Bureau website (bangkoktourist.bma .go.th) for dates.

January *Bangkok International Film Festival* – home-grown talent and overseas indies arrive on the silver screens

February/March *Chinese New Year* – Thai-Chinese celebrate the lunar New Year, with a week of house-cleaning, lion dances and fireworks

March *Kite-Flying Season* – the skies over Sanam Luang and Lumphini Park are filled with colourful, animal-shaped kites

April *Songkhran* – everyone gets wet and wild as water stars in this festival celebrating the Thai lunar New Year

May *Royal Ploughing Ceremony* – His Majesty the King commences rice-planting season at Sanam Luang
Visakha Bucha – Buddha's birth, enlightenment and passing away are honoured with candlelit processions and other merit-making

July *Khao Phansa* – the beginning of the rainy season marks the start of Buddhist Lent, when young men enter the monkhood

September *International Festival of Music & Dance* – an extravaganza of arts and culture is sponsored by the Thailand Cultural Centre
Thailand International Swan-Boat Races – held on Mae Nam Chao Phraya near Rama IX Bridge

October/November *King Chulalongkorn Day* – Rama V is honoured on the anniversary of his death at his revered statue in Dusit (3, E2)
Vegetarian Festival – a ten-day Chinese-Buddhist festival of meatless meals is announced with yellow banners
Ork Phansa – marks the end of the rainy season and Buddhist Lent

November *Loi Krathong* – a beautiful festival where on the night of the full moon, small lotus-shaped boats made of banana leaf containing a lit candle are set adrift on the river
Asiatopia – performance artists from across Southeast Asia converge on Bangkok's public spaces
Bangkok's Pride – a week-long festival of parades, parties and awards is organised by the city's gay businesses and organisations

December *King's Birthday* – locals celebrate their monarch's birthday with lots of twinkling lights

BARS & PUBS

Considering it a form of torture to be isolated from food, Thais typically mix their tippling with nibbling, meaning that most of Bangkok's bars have reliable kitchens.

Bangkok Bar (6, B2)
There's always a fun vibe at this teeny-bopper bar in the heart of Banglamphu. Early on it's a chill little lounge that then shifts into a rowdy hip-hop and pop Petri dish as the crowd seems to self-replicate. And if it is too packed, take refuge next door at Sawadee or cruise over to Th Khao San's unscripted freak show.
☎ 0 2629 4443
✉ 149 Soi Rambutri, Th Chakraphong 🚌 506, 17
🚢 Tha Phra Athit (Banglamphu)
🕑 7pm-2am ♿ fair

Barbican (7, B1) What's a yuppie pub like you doing in a place like this? The sleek Barbican is surrounded on all sides by Thaniya massage parlours, fluent in the tastes of Japanese businessmen. Once you're safely inside, an after-work happy hour mood reigns until closing time.
☎ 0 2234 3590 ✉ 9/4-5 Soi Thaniya, Th Silom
🕑 11.30am-2am
🚉 Sala Daeng ♿ fair

Cheap Charlie's (5, A2)
Wild West meets corporate expat at this quirky wooden beer stall, boasting the cheapest brews on Soi 11. Bangkok becomes a road-tested buddy after you down a few bottles of Singha, sweat through your shirt and argue politics with some know-it-all Euro. Located near the 'Sabai, Sabai Massage' sign.
✉ sub-*soi* off Soi 11, Th Sukhumvit 🕑 5pm-midnight Mon-Sat
🚉 Nana ♿ good

Jool's (5, A2) This surreal British-style pub seats its twisted characters around a horseshoe-shaped bar for impromptu performances. The drunkest usually commandeers the captain's chair while sixty-somethings maul the short-skirted bartenders. A humorous vantage point to observe the sexpat 'locals' taking a breather from nearby Nana Entertainment Plaza.
☎ 0 2252 6413 ✉ Soi 4 (Soi Nana Tai) 🕑 11am-midnight 🚉 Ploenchit or Nana ♿ fair

O'Reilly's (7, B2) A squeaky clean facsimile of an Irish pub, O'Reilly's earns its shamrock for its ever-evolving but affordable happy hour specials. Its central location to other nightspots also makes it a common meeting spot for far-flung friends.
☎ 0 2632 7515
✉ 62/1-2 Th Silom, cnr Soi Thaniya
🕑 11am-1am
🚉 Sala Daeng ♿ fair

Tapas (7, B2) Early in the night, this Moorish-style bar is mellow, with wavering candlelight on the rendered walls. Everyone lies back

Hot in the Town
Bangkok is susceptible to the urban mania of trend-hopping – hip hop, salsa, wine and cigars; what is hot one month is out the next. For the latest, check out *Bangkok Metro* or *Farang,* two city monthlies available on newsstands.

Space efficiency: squeeze into a bar for a cosy meal on Th Phra Athit

against big cushions, picking at tapas and nodding to the chilled-out beats. Later the disco ball starts swirling and the dance floor gets sweaty at this Thai yuppie classic.
☎ 0 2632 0920
✉ 114/7 Silom Soi 4, Th Silom ☼ 10pm-2am
🚇 Sala Daeng ♿ good

Tawandaeng (2, B5)
Looking for a more local feel than your average expat bar? Well, you asked for it: Tawandaeng is a massive beer hall and German-style microbrewery (rong beer). In between stage sets of sing-along pop tunes, choruses of 'Happy Birthday' erupt from the overcrowded tables.
☎ 0 2678 1114
✉ 462/61 Th Phra Ram III, cnr Th Narathiwat Ratchanakarin ☼ 6pm-2am 🚌 taxi ♿ good

Th Khao San (6, B3)
Bangkok's gentrified tourist ghetto is still a human circus of outdoor beer guzzling starring a cast of greasy backpackers, rebellious Thai youths and, of late, moneyed Thais. New dance clubs and upscale bars have added wine, art and class to the mix. The party snakes through to Th Rambutri (6, C3) and Soi Rambutri (6, B2), on either side of Th Chakraphong.
✉ Th Khao San
☼ 6pm-2am 🚌 506, 53, 17 ⚓ Tha Phra Athit (Banglamphu) ♿ good

Th Phra Athit Bars (6, B2)
From the corner opposite the fort to Soi Chana Songkhram, a bouquet of closet-sized bar-restaurants act as communal living rooms for the neighbour-

hood's students and artists. Small plates of food share space with whiskey sets as a squeaky guitar plays all the sing-along favourites.
✉ Th Phra Athit
☼ 4pm-2am 🚌 506, 53 ⚓ Tha Banglamphu ♿ fair

Vertigo (4, F5) True to Bangkok's *Blade Runner* aesthetic, beauty is found high above the teeming streets where the urban jungle appears tranquil. Savour this illusion from the sky-high, open-air perch on the 59th floor of the Banyan Tree Hotel at sunset. For the best views, sit to the right of the bar.
☎ 0 2679 1200
✉ 21/100 Th Sathon Tai, Banyan Tree Hotel
☼ weather permitting
🚇 Surasak 🚌 17, 67

THE SEX INDUSTRY

You wouldn't think that prostitution is illegal in Thailand. Nor would you guess that most of its sex workers cater for Thais, not the foreigners that crowd the go-go bars of Patpong, Thaniya, Nana Entertainment Plaza and Soi Cowboy. But just as appearances can be deceiving, the mythology of Bangkok's sex industry – as a Western-dominated sleazefest established by American GIs – doesn't quite match its history.

Since ancient times, it was a sign of affluence for Thai men to keep mistresses, and many of their first sexual experiences were with prostitutes, considered professionals who spared potential marriage partners from pre-marital pressures. Chinese immigrants set up brothels in Chinatown's notorious Sampeng Lane in the mid-19th century – and these later expanded throughout the country. Prostitution was finally declared illegal in the 1950s but just decades later, as the Vietnam War brought Western men to Bangkok for R&R, a new era of prostitutes catering for foreigners began. The city's first massage parlour opened in Soi Thaniya for Japanese expats (still the *soi*'s biggest customers today) and Thai police officials.

The Patpong area, just a few streets west on Soi Patpong 1 and 2, was originally a banana plantation and became a bar area to cater for stopping-over airline workers. It earned notoriety during the 1980s for its wild sex shows, involving everything from ping-pong balls to razors to midgets on motorbikes.

Today, Soi Cowboy and Nana Entertainment Plaza are the real scenes of sex and love for hire, while Patpong has become a circus sideshow for couples and even families. Although less prolific these days, Patpong voyeurs should be warned of 'free' sex shows where an exorbitant bill appears just as muscle-bound bouncers block your exit. Stick to the first-floor establishments on the main strip where people can enter and leave freely.

DANCE CLUBS

From sleek kittens to mega-watt temples, Bangkok's discos burn strong and bright on certain nights – a visit from a foreign DJ, the music flavour of the month, or the newest player on the scene – then hibernate like sleeping dragons on other nights. Check the city magazines or www .bangkokgigguide.com to see what's on. The cover charge usually includes a drink.

Concept CM2 (4, E2)
This Siam Square club has its bases well and truly covered. There's something for everyone – covers bands belt out funky favourites, giggling gals pretend they're Janet Jackson at the karaoke machine and twinkle-toed types boogie under the disco ball.
☎ 0 2255 6888
✉ Novotel Bangkok on Siam Sq, Soi 6
$ 200B ☼ 7pm-2am
🚇 Siam Square ♿ fair

Lucifer (7, B2) This is no burn-baby-burn disco inferno. Sure, there's a cute papier-mâché devil at the entrance, but Lucifer is a serious club for hardcore techno. Good old Lucifer is also affordable enough to be a hell of a good time almost every night.
☎ 0 2234 6902 ✉ 2nd fl above Radio City, Soi Patpong 1, Th Silom
$ 130B ☼ 8pm-2am
🚇 Sala Daeng ♿ limited

Mystique (5, C1) This Q Bar protégé is perfect for the commitment-shy. Mix and match from the fresh-faced hip-hop on the first floor to the older and wiser electronica scene on the second floor. Or escape it all in the chill-out patio with flickering candles and Latin beats.

Go straight through the first intersection and turn left at the yellow car park sign.
☎ 0 2662 2374
✉ 71/8 Soi 31, Th Sukhumvit $ 600B
☼ 10pm-2am
🚇 Asoke ♿ fair

Narcissus (5, C2) Never has a club been so aptly named. It's mind-boggling to think of the amount of mirror-looking and breathless self-admiration that must have gone on before the designer-label-bedecked young things here could leave the house. Catch a glimpse when a top-shelf DJ is in town.
☎ 0 2258 4805 ✉ btwn Soi 29 & Soi 27, Th Sukhumvit $ 500B
☼ 9pm-2am Sat & Sun
🚇 Asoke ♿ fair

Q Bar (5, A1) Bangkok's 'it' bar has managed to hold on to such a fickle title

The ever-popular Q Bar

since its nearly pre-historic opening in 1999. This darkened industrial space is decorated by movie stars slouching into the dark padded-leather walls, socialites traipsing upstairs to the outdoor balcony or adventurous lushes spending quality time with the drinks menu.
☎ 0 2252 3274
✉ 34 Soi 11, Th Sukhumvit $ 600B Fri & Sat
☼ 8pm-2am 🚇 Nana ♿ fair

Flying Solo
If you've ascended to the City of Angels without a companion, then make two distinct lines. Men over here in line A; women, line B.

Line A: Welcome to paradise, where beautiful women will throw themselves at you, all for a modest sum (either monetary or status). Line B: For better or worse, you will be virtually invisible except at a few neighbourhood spots: Jool's (p85), Ad Here and Cheap Charlie's (p85).

LIVE MUSIC

Grade-A jazz musicians make an honoured stop in several of Bangkok's hotels. Other-genre musicians let their hair hang down in Bangkok's elbow-tight rock-and-roll clubs.

Ad Here the 13th (6, C1)
The best little dive bar in Thailand, Ad Here is a homey meeting place to have too many late nights and countless suds and cigs. The house band steered by guitarist Pong and vocalist Georgia melt the night and the regulars' hearts with smoking blues tunes and rocking classics.
✉ 13 Th Samsen
☽ music starts 10pm
🚍 30 ⚓ Tha Phra Athit (Banglamphu) ♿ fair

Bamboo Bar (3, E9)
You could be forgiven for thinking that Thailand was a Brit colony when you visit the Bamboo Bar, the city's top jazz spot. Patrons sip G&Ts while lounging in leopard-skin chairs, feeling a million miles away from the heat and dust, while jazz bands or singers soothe any remaining tensions.
☎ 0 2236 0400
✉ Oriental Hotel, 48 Soi Oriental, Th Charoen Krung ☽ 11am-2am Fri & Sat, 11am-1am Sun-Thu
🚍 Saphan Taksin ⚓ Tha Oriental or hotel shuttle boat from Tha Sathon ♿ good

Brown Sugar (4, F4)
Evoking the intimacy of New Orleans jazz clubs, this compact bar lends an ear to be-bop and ragtime, leaving the smooth sounds to the hotel lobbies. On Sunday nights, the high-powered musicians who are touring the luxury hotels assemble here for impromptu jam sessions.
☎ 0 2250 1826
✉ 231/20 Th Sarasin
☽ 5pm-2am
🚍 Chitlom ♿ fair

Cafe Democ (3, C4)
Serious fans of electronica (trance and its cousins) love this bar and its beats. But the platters make groove-worthy revolutions when DJ Spydamonkee or overseas guests are in orbit. Keep an eye out for their appearances, otherwise you'll find the term 'spinning' has been lost in translation.
☎ 0 2622 2571
✉ 78 Th Ratchadamnoen Klang ☽ 4pm-2am Tue-Sun 🚍 503, 506, 509, 511 ♿ fair

Living Room (5, B2) We'll come clean – the Living Room is a hotel buffet restaurant. But where most of its ilk are sedated by corny covers bands, this cosy upmarket place is alive with the grooves of some of the top jazz acts around. The mellow Sunday brunch starts at around 11am.
☎ 0 2653 0333
✉ Sheraton Grande Sukhumvit, 250 Th Sukhumvit, btwn Sois 12 & 14
☽ 9pm-midnight
🚍 Asoke ♿ fair

Saxophone (2, B4)
Saxophone is still Bangkok's premier live music venue, a dark, intimate space where you can pull up a chair just a few metres away from the band and see their every bead of sweat. If you like some mystique in your musicians, watch the blues, jazz, reggae or rock from the balcony.
☎ 0 2246 5472
✉ 3/8 Th Phayathai, Victory Monument
☽ 6pm-2am 🚍 Victory Monument ♿ good

Jazzin' at the Bamboo Bar

CINEMAS

When it is hot and steamy outside, Bangkok's plush cinemas are a welcome escape. Dozens of cinemas screen movies in English, with Thai subtitles; check the *Bangkok Post* or www.movieseer.com for session times. Tickets cost around 100B for basic stadium seating and up to 500B for VIP luxury. The Thai national anthem is played before every movie screening and patrons are expected to stand respectfully.

Alliance Française (4, F5)
If you feel like some intensity, check out the French movies (with English subtitles). Keep an eye on the Alliance Française website to see what's showing.
☎ 0 2670 4200
💻 www.alliance-francaise.or.th ✉ 29 Th Sathon Tai 🚇 Sala Daeng 🚌 17, 67 ♿ good ♿

EGV Grand (4, D2) Place your snack order on the way in, wait until after the royal anthem to recline your sofa chair to horizontal and snuggle in for the long haul. Try not to fall asleep before your food arrives.
☎ 0 2812 9999
✉ 6th fl, Siam Discovery Center, Th Phra Ram I
💲 300B 🚇 Siam Square ♿ good ♿

Goethe Institute (4, G5)
Expats and film buffs catch the regular screenings of German-language films and retrospectives at this cultural centre. You don't have to speak German, as the films have English subtitles, and there's a great beer garden for a drink before, during or after a show.
☎ 0 2287 0726
💻 www.goethe.de/bangkok ✉ 18/1 Soi Goethe, Th Sathon Tai 🚇 Sala Daeng 🚌 17, 67 ♿ good ♿

Enjoy star treatment at the EGV Grand

SF Cinema (5, D2)
On the very top floor of the Emporium shopping centre, this cinema serves up the usual Hollywood shoot-and-snog standards. But this cinema stands out because of its fab sound and projection quality.
☎ 0 2260 9333
✉ The Emporium, 6th fl, Th Sukhumvit, btwn Soi 22 & 24 🚇 Phrom Phong ♿ good ♿

SF Cinema City (4, D2)
Grab a big box of popcorn and find a seat among the Thai teenagers waiting to see the latest blockbuster. If that sounds like your worst nightmare, spend the extra cash and buy one of the gold-class seats.
☎ 0 2611 6444 ✉ 7th fl, Mah Boon Krong, cnr Th Phra Ram I & Th Phayathai 🚇 National Stadium ♿ good ♿

Tollywood or Bust
If you've got your eye on the silver screen, Thailand is emerging as an art-movie darling. Keep an eye out for new releases from the reigning Midas of Thai cinema, Nonzee Nimibutr; the MTV-fuelled Danny and Oxide Pang brothers; and Cannes winners Pen-Ek Ratanaruang and Apichatpong Weerasethakul. Bangkok's International Film Festival (p84) provides a screening room for Thai talent, as do art houses like **Lido** (4, D2; ☎ 0 2252 6498; Siam Square, Th Phra Ram I; Skytrain Siam Square), **Scala** (4, D2; ☎ 0 2251 2861; Siam Square Soi 1, Th Phra Ram I; Skytrain Siam Square) and **House** (2, C4; UMG Building, RCA, Th Phra Ram IX; subway Rama IX).

TRADITIONAL MUSIC, THEATRE & DANCE

There are a lot of very average, made-for-tourist cultural shows in Bangkok. For the 'real deal', try to catch one of these highly regarded *khon* (masked drama), *lákhon* (traditional folk tales, often sung) or puppet performances.

Chalermkrung Royal Theatre (3, C5) This restored Thai Deco building – also known as Sala Chaloem Krung – hosts *khon* performances as well as modern Thai-language drama. Here *khon* is a high-tech production, with a flash audio system and computer-generated laser graphics. Dress respectfully (no shorts, sleeveless tops or sandals).
☎ 0 2222 0434 ✉ cnr Th Charoen Krung & Th Triphet 🚌 501, 507, 508 🚢 Tha Saphan Phut ♿ fair 🚹

Joe Louis Puppet Theatre (4, G5) The ancient art of Thai puppetry *(lákhon lék)* was rescued by the late Sakorn Yangkhiawsod, more popularly known as Joe Louis, in 1985. Today Joe's children carry on the tradition, presenting elaborate performances of *Ramakian* and Thai myths. Bookings recommended.
☎ 0 2252 9683 🖥 www.joelouis-theater .com ✉ Suan Lum Night Bazaar, cnr Th Phra Ram IV & Th Withayu 💲 600B 🕐 show 7.30pm 🚌 13, 14, 115 🚇 Lumphini ♿ good 🚹

National Theatre (6, A3) The National Theatre has kept *khon* dance-drama alive through its slumps in popularity. Originally only performed for the royal court, *khon* depicts scenes from *Ramakian*. You can also catch a *lákhon* show here. Pick up a schedule from the Bangkok Tourist Bureau (p121).
☎ 0 2224 0171 ✉ 2 Th Ratchini 💲 50-200B 🚌 511, 53 🚢 Tha Mahathat ♿ fair 🚹

Patravadi Theatre (3, A4) Next to Supatra River House, Patravadi is Bangkok's only open-air theatre and one of its most avant-garde. Led by Patravadi Mejudhon, a famous Thai actor and playwright, the troupe's performances blend traditional Thai dance and themes with modern choreography and modern music and costume.
☎ 0 2412 7287 🖥 www.patravadi theatre.com ✉ Soi Wat Rakhang, Thonburi 💲 300-800B 🕐 shows 7pm Fri-Sun 🚢 private cross-river ferry from Tha Maharat ♿ good 🚹

Sala Rim Naam (3, E9) The riverside Sala Rim Naam, a stunning Thai pavilion made of teak, marble and bronze, holds nightly classical dance performances which are far superior to the average tourist fare. It's part of the Oriental Hotel (just across the river). Bookings recommended.
☎ 0 2437 6211 ✉ Oriental Hotel, 48 Soi Oriental, Th Charoen Krung 💲 1600B 🕐 7-10pm 🚢 free shuttle boat from Oriental Hotel ♿ good 🚹

Get a dose of dance-drama in your veins at the National Theatre

GAY & LESBIAN BANGKOK

Lady-boy stage shows and pretty boy discos, centred on Soi 4 and Soi 2 off Th Silom, are favourites of money boys (prostitutes) and wallet-worthy Westerners. The Thai gay professionals typically rendezvous at the city's fashionable restaurants or changing venues on the outskirts of the city. But when dance fever strikes, everyone (regardless of orientation) heads to Silom. Lesbians *(tom-dee)* don't claim a singular hang-out but mix in the bars along Th Phra Athit (p86) and in Silom's gay spots.

Balcony (7, B2) Balcony is your classic all-round, good-time bar, where hotpants and string vests check out the talent and tables of straight couples order countless rounds. A table outside under the red lanterns is the prime position for watching the passing parade.
☎ 0 2235 5891
✉ 8/6-8 Th Silom Soi 4, Th Silom ⏱ 5pm-2am
🚇 Sala Daeng
Ⓜ Silom 🖐 good

Coffee Society (7, B2) At the nexus of Bangkok's Pink Triangle, Coffee Society serves as a community centre hosting art displays, informal conferences and caffeine-laced cruising.
☎ 0 2235 9784
✉ 18 Th Silom
⏱ 8am-4am Mon-Sat, 10am-4am Sun
🚇 Sala Daeng ♿ good

Short pants or hot pants?

DJ Station (7, C2) Neo-industrial DJ Station is a long-standing dance club in a town that loves change. The music varies wildly from handbag to hard house but the dance floor remains packed with shirtless sweaty boys.
☎ 0 2266 4029
✉ 8/6-8 Soi 2, Th Silom
⏱ 10pm-2am 💲 300B cover 🚇 Sala Daeng
Ⓜ Silom 🖐 fair

Expresso (7, C2) Expresso looks too cool for its own good, but don't take that as a bad thing in manic Soi 2. Its relative calm and sophistication is good news for those who can't take the noise and crowds of the big clubs. Lots of looking goes on through the floor-to-ceiling windows.
☎ 0 2632 7223 ✉ Soi 2, Th Silom ⏱ 6pm-2am
🚇 Sala Daeng
Ⓜ Silom 🖐 fair

Freeman (7, B2) Reputedly the best cabaret in town, Freeman's midnight shows are a little raunchier than the typical tourist-oriented shows of Broadway homage and pink prom dresses.
☎ 0 2632 8032 ✉ on the small soi btwn Soi 2 & Soi Thaniya, Th Silom
⏱ 10pm-2am 🚇 Sala Daeng Ⓜ Silom ♿ fair

JJ Park (7, C2) Guppies (gay yuppies) have claimed a niche amid the usual suspects on Soi 2 at this camp shack famous for its drag shows. Regulars also recommend the live music and comedy shows.
☎ 0 2233 3247
✉ 8/3 Soi 2, Th Silom
⏱ 10pm-2am 🚇 Sala Daeng Ⓜ Silom 🖐 fair

Telephone (7, B2) Muscle boys and queens parade past Telephone's outdoor tables, taking in the scene at one of Bangkok's oldest and most popular gay bars. Inside, all the tables have a telephone you can use to call any patrons you fancy.
☎ 0 2234 3279
✉ 114/11-13 Silom Soi 4, Th Silom ⏱ 5pm-2am
🚇 Sala Daeng
Ⓜ Silom 🖐 good

Vega (5, D1) This casual, lesbian-owned restaurant-pub pours such powerful cocktails that the cliquish tables of friends can no longer resist the urge to kick up their heels. Friday and Saturday nights, you might rub shoulders with local lesbian celebrities.
☎ 0 2258 8273
✉ 32/1 Soi 39, Th Sukhumvit ⏱ 6pm-midnight
🚇 Phrom Phong
♿ good

SPECTATOR SPORTS

Bangkokians are not the most sporty (bit hard, considering the lack of recreation space) but they do have their favourite spectator sports.

For two Sundays a month, the **Royal Bangkok Sports Club** (4, E3; ☎ 02-251 018186; 1 Th Henri Dunant; Skytrain Ratchadamri) is a frenzy of furious betting, drinking and horse-racing. Usually the domain of members (and there is a whopping waiting list), the club opens its doors to the great unwashed for the races. The other main racing venue is the **Royal Turf Club** (3, F3; ☎ 0 2628 1810; 183 Th Phitsanulok; bus No 509), not far from Chitlada Palace. It hosts Bangkok's biggest horse race, the King's Cup, around the first or second week of January as well as regular races on alternative Sundays at the RBSC.

Maybe Bangkok's passion for soccer stems from the old Siamese football, or *tàkrâw*. Players usually stand around in a circle and kick a woven rattan ball soccer-style, trying to keep it airborne and earning points for the style, difficulty and variety of their kicking manoeuvres. In international competition (the Thais introduced the sport to the South East Asian Games and, with the Malaysians, have dominated it) *tàkrâw* is played like volleyball, except only the feet and head may touch the ball. There aren't that many regular professional games played, but go to Lumphini Park and you'll probably see an impromptu match.

The most dynamic and exciting Thai sport is *muay thai,*

> ### It's Got a Ring to It
> When a Thai boxer is ready for the ring, he is given a fighting name – usually a none-too-subtle reminder of how much pain these guys aim to inflict. Just so you know what you might be in for, a recent session at Lumphini stadium boasted clashes like: Dangerous Uneven-Legged Man vs the Bloody Elbow; the Human Stone vs the King of the Knee; and No Mercy Killer vs the Golden Left Leg.

or Thai boxing, considered by many to be the ultimate in hand-to-hand fighting. Matches can be violent, but the surrounding spectacle of crazy music, pre-match rituals and manic betting is worth the ticket price.

Fights are held at **Ratchadamnoen Boxing Stadium** (3, E3; ☎ 0 2281 4205; Th Ratchadamnoen Nok, Dusit; bus No 503, 509) and **Lumphini Boxing Stadium** (4, G5; ☎ 0 2251 4303; Th Phra Ram IV, near Th Withayu; subway Lumphini). Ratchadamnoen fights are on Monday, Wednesday and Thursday at 6pm, and Sunday at 5pm, while Lumphini hosts them on Tuesday, Friday and Saturday at 6pm. Tickets cost 500/800/1500B (3rd class/2nd class/ringside) – always buy from the ticket windows. The stadiums don't usually fill up until the main event, at around 8pm.

Sleeping

Bangkok has always known how to look after its visitors. In the days of steamer travel, the Oriental Hotel was the home-away-from-home of choice for adventurous artists and writers, like Somerset Maugham who spent months there recovering from a bout of malaria. During and after the Vietnam War, American soldiers R&R'd in hotels named after cities back home like Reno and Miami, while travellers on the overland hippy trail crashed at guesthouses around Soi Ngam Duphli. These days, visitors are more likely to hit the sack in the famous backpackers' ghetto of Th Khao San or live it up on a package holiday to luxury hotels.

If there's one legacy of the Asian economic boom, besides empty apartment blocks, it's the business focus of the top-end and deluxe hotels. Even a room that appears to be a temple to relaxation will have a desk and facilities like direct-dial phones and modem connections. It's rare for one of these luxury hotels not to have a top-notch business centre.

Business travellers tend to stay in the white-collar districts of Silom and Sukhumvit, districts also favoured by lone male travellers for their proximity to 'entertainment' districts like Patpong, Nana Entertainment Plaza and Soi Cowboy. Siam Square is convenient for shopaholics. If you want to live cheaply or escape the skyscrapers, you're better off making a camp in Banglamphu – many of the must-sees are within walking or boating distance, and the area enjoys a more peaceful, riverside location. Devoid of pushy tailors or *túk-túk* drivers, Chinatown has become the 'adventurous' travellers' outpost.

Standards, luxury and views are phenomenal at the city's deluxe and top-end hotels. The mid-range options, especially around lower Sukhumvit, vary right from superb to disturbed; the hotels listed in this book are true standouts. The budget range offers stripped down basics that foster a youth hostel spirit in the communal spaces.

Room Rates

The categories indicate the cost per night of a standard double room, including all tax and service charges, during the high season.

Deluxe	over 10,000B (US$238)
Top End	4200-9954B (US$100-237)
Mid-Range	1000-4999B (US$23-99)
Budget	under 999B (US$22)

DELUXE

Banyan Tree (4, F5) This little sister of the legendary Phuket retreat is the most touchy-feely of Bangkok's deluxe hotels, where oil-burner scents and New Age music blend seamlessly with the sleek modern Asian design. Skip the tiny pool and head for the sanctuary of your suite or the day spa (p43).
☎ 0 2679 1200
🖥 www.banyantree.com
✉ 21/100 Th Sathon Tai
🚇 Surasak 🚌 17, 67
♿ good 🍴 Bai Yun

Conrad Hotel (4, G3) Media, moguls and models of every nationality live large at this moderne abode. Decorated with Thai silks and rich earth tones, Conrad flunks out on service but aces the bathroom-cum-spa trend with deep soak tubs and overhead 'rain' showerheads. No need to wander far for your nightly bubbly; the in-hotel Diplomat Bar is every bilingual's favourite engagement.
☎ 0 2690 9999
🖥 www.conradhotels.com
✉ 87 Th Withayu
🚇 Ploenchit ♿ good
🍴 Club 87

Grand Hyatt Erawan (4, F2) Every room in this imposing neoclassical edifice is an art gallery, right down to the originals in your suite's loo. But that's just one bonus of staying here: what about the shopping centres just a credit-card swipe away?
☎ 0 2254 1234
🖥 www.bangkok.hyatt.com
✉ cnr Th Ratchadamri & Th Ploenchit
🚇 Chitlom ♿ good
🍴 Spasso

Intercontinental Bangkok (4, F2) Next door to *haute couture* shopping, the Intercontinental (formerly Le Meridien President Hotel & Tower) is a worthy modern scraper for a post retail nap. Standard rooms are dressed up with huge beds, marble bathrooms, and a separate tub and shower (tall enough for over-sized foreigners).
☎ 0 2656 0444
🖥 www.intercontinental.com
✉ 973 Th Ploenchit
🚇 Chitlom ♿ good
🍴 Shin Daikoku

Oriental Hotel (3, E9) The Sir James A Michener suite gives an inkling of why this establishment is one of the world's most famous hotels. Sir James liked his writing desk overlooking the river and an enormous red claw-foot bath in the bathroom – testament to the Oriental's enduring philosophies of timeless style and service above and beyond the call of duty.
☎ 0 2659 9000
🖥 www.mandarinoriental.com

Above and beyond: the Oriental Hotel

✉ 48 Soi Oriental, Th Charoen Krung 🚇 Saphan Taksin 🚌 75, 115, 116 ⛴ Tha Oriental or hotel shuttle boat from Tha Sathon/Saphan Taksin Skytrain ♿ good ✗ Le Normandie (p80)

Peninsula Hotel (4, A6)
Yet another darling in Bangkok's luxury clique, the sister of Hong Kong's legendary Peninsula has sweeping views from a rare vantage point, Thonburi. While it might lack the Oriental's classic appeal, it more than makes up for it with modern toys such as bathroom televisions featuring condensation-free screens, a 60m swimming pool and a helipad.
☎ 0 2861 2888
🖥 www.peninsula.com

Staying for a While?
Serviced apartments with daily cleaning, sports facilities and city views are concentrated in the business district of Silom, near embassy row on Lang Suan and along Sukhumvit. If you're not riding the cushy corporate expense account, you might want to be more tenacious in finding wallet-friendly options. Reasonable monthly stays are available at hotels like La Résidence Hotel & Serviced Apartments (p100), Wendy House (p102) and Pathumwan House (p100).

✉ 333 Th Charoen Nakhon, Thonburi ⛴ hotel shuttle boat from Tha Sathon ♿ limited ✗ Mei Jiang (p80)

Sukhothai Hotel (4, F5)
Designed by Edward Tuttle, the creative hand behind Phuket's heavenly Amanpuri resort, the Sukhothai Hotel is a low-rise temple to Asian minimalism. The Sukhothai-era-inspired artworks inside the rooms, around the expansive gardens and in the still ponds are reminders of Tuttle's inspiration – Thailand's first kingdom of Sukhothai.
☎ 0 2287 0222
🖥 www.sukhothai.com ✉ 13/3 Th Sathon Tai 🚌 15, 67 ♿ good ✗ Celadon (p77)

Put away that paddle; not Bangkok's worst flood, just an ornamental pool at the Sukhothai Hotel

TOP END

Amari Airport Hotel

(2, C1) The rooms are tired and overpriced but you can't beat the location, location, location. Geared specifically towards the transit traveller, who can book in for a three-hour mini-stay or watch departure and arrival schedules on TV, this hotel is an easy stumble across a walkway from the Don Muang airport (the international airport until the new Suvanabhumi Airport is completed).
☎ 0 2566 1020
🖳 www.amari.com
✉ 333 Th Chert Wudthakas (enter via walkway from terminal 1)
🚹 good 🍴 Arriva Café

Amari Watergate Hotel

(4, E1) As you'd expect of a flagship hotel, the Watergate is a sophisticated embodiment of all that the home-grown Amari chain stands for: good management, Thai-inspired design, friendly service and a willingness to go the extra yards to cater for families and disabled travellers.
☎ 0 2653 9000
🖳 www.amari.com
✉ 847 Th Phetchaburi
🚇 505, 511, 512
🛶 khlong taxi to Tha Pratunam 🚹 good
🍴 Grappino (p75)

Bangkok Marriott Resort & Spa

(2, A5) Set amid lushly landscaped gardens by the river, the Marriott really is that clichéd place where you can get away from it all – home, hassles and even Bangkok. You can

either laze about the divine poolside area or indulge in a Manohra Rice Barge Dinner Cruise (p52).
☎ 0 2476 0022
🖳 www.marriott hotels.com/bkkth
✉ 257 Th Charoen Nakhon, Thonburi
🛥 hotel shuttle boat from Tha Sathon, Tha Oriental & Tha River City
🚹 good 🍴 Trader Vic's

Four Seasons Hotel

(4, F2) Service is the undoubted cornerstone of the recently rechristened Four Seasons (formerly the Regent). All the necessities, just a phone call away, keep jet-lagged business-people from melting under deadlines. And old-world style comes just as effortlessly – just try high tea in the lobby, complete with a string quartet. It should be noted, though, that the hotel's standard rooms are situated around an outdoor (non-air-conditioned) courtyard.
☎ 0 2250 1000
🖳 www.fourseasons.com
✉ 155 Th Ratchadamri
🚇 Ratchadamri 🚹 good
🍴 The Lobby

Landmark Bangkok

(5, A2) The revolving entry door here hasn't stopped turning, thanks to a business centre that never sleeps and staff who understand corporate culture. But now with the Skytrain only a three-minute walk away, package holidaymakers are also appreciating the luxuriously practical Landmark.
☎ 0 2254 0404
🖳 www.landmark bangkok.com
✉ 138 Th Sukhumvit, btwn Sois 4 & 6 🚇 Nana
🚹 good 🍴 Nipa Thai

Novotel Bangkok on Siam Square

(4, E2) The Novotel is in quite a nifty position if you're in

Base camp for the serious shopper: the Novotel

Mouth music: buffet lunch at the Sheraton Grande in Sukhumvit

Bangkok for the shopping. It's located within walking or Skytraining distance of the big centres, like MBK, Siam Discovery Center and Gaysorn Plaza, and is one of the cheapest top-end accommodation options available.
☎ 0 2255 6888
🖥 www.novotel.com
✉ Soi 6, Siam Sq
🚈 Siam Square
♿ good ✗ Focazzia

Raffles Nai Lert Park (4, G1) Formerly an outpost of the Hilton chain, this highly ranked hotel has changed hands (and names) to the Raffles International group. What does remain is the exquisite garden with a private jogging track and a tropically landscaped pool providing an instant elixir to jet lag. Room renovations (and hopefully service too) were in progress at writing.
☎ 0 2253 0123
🖥 www.swissotel.com
✉ 2 Th Withayu
🚈 Ploenchit 🛥 khlong taxi to Tha Withayu
♿ good

Shangri-La Hotel (4, A6) The firmly family-friendly Shangri-La had long been

one of the world's top hotels when it built the glamorous Krung Thep wing, where the rooms open onto a spacious balcony overflowing with magenta bougainvillea and, if they're west-facing, a lofty river vista. Now, the competition is tougher than ever.
☎ 0 2236 7777
🖥 www.shangri-la.com
✉ 89 Soi Wat Suan Phlu, Th Charoen Krung
🚈 Saphan Taksin
🛥 Tha Sathon 🚌 75, 115, 116 ♿ good
✗ Angelini (p79)

Sheraton Grande Sukhumvit (5, B2) Decisions, decisions. Do you recline thoughtfully on cushions in the shade of a poolside *sala*, check into the dark and intimate day spa-to-die-for (p43) or snap your fingers to world-class jazz on offer in the Living Room bar (p89)? High-class relaxation can be tough.
☎ 0 2649 8888
🖥 www.sheraton grandesukhumvit.com
✉ 250 Th Sukhumvit, btwn Sois 12 & 14
🚈 Asoke ♿ good
✗ Living Room (p89)

Swiss Lodge (7, B2) Don't be fooled by the name – there's not a cuckoo clock in sight at this classy boutique hotel situated in the heart of the Silom district. With only 57 rooms, it is a quiet, well-managed option for both businesspeople and couples. However, Swiss enthusiasts shouldn't despair: fondue is a speciality of the in-house restaurant.
☎ 0 2233 5345
🖥 www.swisslodge.com
✉ 3 Th Convent
🚈 Sala Daeng ♿ limited
✗ Café Swiss

Westin Grande Sukhumvit (5, B2) This boxy beast has been transformed from dowdy to corporate. The trademarked 'Heavenly' beds are divinely soft and cosy, and the bathrooms are friendly to the average giants among us. The package is even more attractive with a generous discount.
☎ 0 2651 1000
🖥 www.westin.com /bangkok
✉ 259 Th Sukhumvit at Soi 19
🚈 Asoke ♿ good
✗ Horizon Sky Lounge & Karaoke

MID-RANGE

Bangkok Christian Guesthouse (7, C2)

A Christian guesthouse just a short stroll from sex-for-sale Patpong and Thaniya? This place's many fans like its atmosphere of calm amid the craziness. Set in a big garden, it will be an excellent option for austerity and play space for the kids.

☎ 0 2233 6303
🖳 www.bcgh.org
✉ 123 Soi 2, Th Convent
🚉 Sala Daeng ♿ good
🍴 Eat Me (p77)

Buddy Lodge (6, C3)

A stylish boutique on Khao San? If you met Khao San in its gangly teen years, you'll be astonished to see its coming of age. Swanky Buddy Lodge has charming rooms and the usual suspects of incongruously grungy backpackers.

☎ 0 2629 4477
🖳 www.buddylodge.com
✉ 265 Th Khao San
🚤 Tha Phra Athit (Banglamphu)
🚌 506, 53 ♿ limited
🍴 Buddy Beer Bar

Federal Hotel (5, A2)

Well-known in sexpat circles as 'Club Fed', this former Vietnam-era rest and relaxation stop has tidied up enough to be good value in a neighbourhood of disappointments. Set up a base in one of the comfortable upstairs rooms, lounge around the frangipani-ringed pool or revive the days of Motown in their American-style coffee shop. Ship out if offered a mouldy ground-level room.

☎ 0 2253 0175
🖳 federalhotel@hotmail.com ✉ 27 Soi 11, Th Sukhumvit
🚉 Nana ♿ limited
🍴 Federal Coffee Shop

Fortuna Hotel (5, A2)

Near Little Arabia, this modest number surprises guests with a shot of personality;

Booking Lines

Promotions abound in Bangkok's hotel world. The following chains offer discounts through their websites; you can also find home-country reservation numbers online.

Amari (www.amari.com)

Mandarin Oriental (www.mandarinoriental.com)

Marriott (Marriott.com)

Shangri-La (www.shangri-la.com)

Sheraton (www.sheraton.com)

Summit Hotels & Resorts (Landmark) (www.summithotels.com)

not the typical ho-hum décor. Lots of business-people fill the ledgers, sporting an air of middle management. The girlie-bar scene is just steps away but it is easy to ignore what does traipse through the doors. ☎ 0 2251 5121 🖥 www.fortuna bangkok.com ✉ 19 Soi 5, Th Sukhumvit 🚇 Ploen-chit & Nana ♿ good ✗ Nasir al-Masri (p73)

La Résidence Hotel & Serviced Apartments (4, C5) Boutique without flash, La Résidence does the 'inn' thing. Its 26 rooms are individually decorated in bright and cheerful styles, and the compact layout is a nice break from the monotony of endless hotel hallways. Hanging out in the Silom area, La Residence also offers monthly rentals. ☎ 0 2233 3301 🖥 www.laresidence bangkok.com ✉ 173/8-9 Th Surawong 🚇 Chong Nonsi 🚌 75, 115 ♿ limited ✗ Somboon Seafood (p78)

Majestic Suites (3, H2) Majestic seems too grand a name for such an intimate hotel with stylish rooms

and top-notch security. But the location – a step off Th Sukhumvit and a stroll from the Skytrain – is certainly princely. ☎ 0 2656 8220 🖥 www.majesticsuites .com ✉ 110-110/1 Th Sukhumvit (btwn Sois 4 & 6) 🚇 Nana ♿ limited ✗ The Atlanta Coffee Shop (p72)

Pathumwan House (4, D1) Tucked way back in the crook of the *soi*, this high-rise is primarily a long-term business hotel with monthly and weekly rates, but lots of short-termers have scouted out this bargain. Rooms are a decent size with wet bar and a generous bed. In the front courtyard, a collection of caged birds sing to whoever will listen. ☎ 0 2612 3580 ✉ 22 Soi Kasem San 1, Th Phra Ram 🚇 National Stadium 🛥 *khlong* taxi to Tha Ratchathewi ♿ limited ✗ Sorn's (p76)

Pinnacle Hotel (4, G5) Thanks to the new subway, prim and proper Pinnacle is tops for travellers headed to the convention centre or nearby embassies. And

for Bangkok juxtaposition, this neighbourhood was the city's first shoestringers' crash pad before ceding the crown to Th Khao San. ☎ 0 2287 0111 ✉ 17 Soi Ngam Duphli, Th Phra Ram IV 🚇 Lumphini 🚌 507, 115 ♿ good ✗ Sara-Jane's (p78)

Royal Asia Lodge & Paradise (5, B2) Compared to the other ageing mid-range hotels in Sukhumvit, Royal Asia could be called a spring chicken. Hardly showing the wear and tear of clumsy visitors, Royal Asia further defies the ageing process by being well-removed from the chaos with a peaceful location right at the end of a residential *soi*. ☎ 0 2251 5514 🖥 www.royalasialodge .com ✉ 91 Soi 8, Th Sukhumvit 🚇 Nana ♿ limited ✗ Crepes & Co (p72)

Royal Hotel (6, B3) An old Bangkok faithful with a marble lobby that echoes with Muzak tinkles, the Royal is a handy jumping-off point for a Ratanakosin ramble, temple crawl or just a laze around Sanam Luang.

Boom, Boom, Boom? Not in my Room!

As you've no doubt noticed, the sex industry permeates every aspect of Bangkok tourism, and lodging is the closest intersection of an average tourist with one of Bangkok's many sex tourists. All hotels on lower Sukhumvit (between Soi 1 and Soi 21/Asoke) host visitors who have one itinerary – go to the hostess bars and return to the room with a girl. Only the Atlanta Hotel (p102) openly forbids bar girls. How will this affect you? Morally and aesthetically it might be annoying; you might even be mildly disturbed by some next-door noises. But from a voyeuristic per-spective, you can't watch this kind of behaviour at home.

Don't expect to run into these two in the lift, even at the Royal Hotel

Most taxi drivers know it as 'Ratanakosin'.
☎ 0 2222 9111
✉ cnr Th Ratchadamnoen Klang & Th Atsadang
🚌 511, 512, 15, 60, 15
♿ good ✕ Royal Hotel Coffee Shop

Siam Orchid Inn (4, F2)
Opposite Central World Plaza, Siam Orchid is a petite anomaly in a super-sized neighbourhood. Well-appointed rooms boast all the standard amenities and are decorated with Thai reproduction antiques.
☎ 0 2255 3140 🖥 siam _orchidinn@hotmail.com

✉ 109 Soi Ratchadamri, Th Ratchadamri
🚇 Chitlom ♿ good
✕ Foodloft (p75)

Viengtai Hotel (6, C2)
Viengtai is all cool, marbled reticence surrounded by the Khao San madness. Once you're settled in your air-conditioned comfort zone, you will appreciate the proximity and the retreat afforded by the bump up in the budget category.
☎ 0 2280 5434 🖥 www .viengtai.co.th ✉ 42 Th Tani (entrance on Th Rambutri) 🚌 506, 53

⚓ Tha Phra Athit (Banglamphu) ♿ good
✕ Shoshana's (p69)

White Orchid Hotel (3, E6)
Smack-bang in the middle of the Chinatown action, this hotel's rooms are clean and good value. Just don't expect to launch forays into Silom or Sukhumvit from here – Chinatown constitutes its own inescapable fun house.
☎ 0 2226 0026
✉ 409-21 Th Yaowarat
🚌 501, 507, 73, 53
⚓ Tha Ratchawong
♿ limited
✕ Shangarila (p71)

BUDGET

Anna's Café & Bed (7, C3)

If you need to crash like a backpacker but you also want to keep up the appearance of a business executive, then Anna's is your gal. This guesthouse, euphemistically called a 'boutique B&B', has plain and simple dorms, private rooms with en suite bathrooms and a family room that is large enough to sleep four.

☎ 0 2632 1323
✉ 44/16 Th Convent
🚇 Sala Daeng
♿ limited
✕ Anna's Café

Atlanta (5, A3)

The lobby of this retro institution is such a 1950s classic – with jazz streaming from the speakers, writing desks equipped with fans and a time-capsuled café – that a cult of devotees overlook the frustratingly weary condition of the rooms. Have a look both at the rooms and the outdoor pool (another clincher) before you commit yourself.

☎ 0 2252 6069
🖥 www.theatlanta hotel.bizland.com
✉ 78 Soi 2, Th Sukhumvit
🚇 Nana ♿ limited
✕ Atlanta Coffee Shop (p72)

Burapha Hotel (3, D5)

Near Phahurat, Burapha is a favourite of the grass-roots importer-exporters from neighbouring countries and boasts several storeys offering clean, simple rooms. You won't be able to get in and out of this neighbourhood in a hurry, but there are aimless, atmospheric rambles to be enjoyed in endless abundance.

☎ 0 2221 3545
✉ 160/14 Th Charoen Krung
🚌 501, 507, 53, 73
⚓ Tha Saphan Phut
♿ good
✕ Royal India (p72)

Malaysia Hotel (4, G5)

Tidy and attractively priced, Malaysia is accommodation best suited to the thrifty and the tolerant who might find themselves amused by the primary clientele – Western gay sexpats. High-school hormones may be ricocheting around the hotel lobby, but the rooms are some of the cleanest in the price range.

☎ 0 2286 3582
✉ 54 Soi Ngam Duphli, Th Phra Ram IV
🚇 Lumphini
🚌 507, 13, 74, 115
♿ limited
✕ Malaysia Coffee Shop

Niagara (4, D5)

Tucked away in a quiet street not far from Th Silom, Niagara is plain but amazingly good value. The halls might seem a little institutional; however, for a modest price you get clean rooms with a TV (complimentary porn), a bathroom and air con.

☎ 0 2233 5783/4
✉ 26 Soi Seuksa Withaya, Th Silom 🚇 Chong Nonsi
🚌 502, 15, 67
♿ limited ✕ Soi 20 Food Market (p78)

Wendy House (4, D1)

Refreshingly low key and centrally located, Wendy House would easily win any Miss Congeniality competition. The karmic balance of conscientious cleaning and friendly staff is rewarded with tidy, early-to-bed guests. No lift.

☎ 0 2216 2436
✉ 36/2 Soi Kasem San 1, Th Phra Ram I
🚇 National Stadium
⚓ *khlong* taxi to Tha Ratchathewi ♿ limited
✕ Sorn's (p76)

Travelling with Children

It's a rare Bangkok hotel – but there are a few – that doesn't like hosting children. Even at the fanciest hotels, you'll probably find it hard to stop the staff playing with your kids. At most mid-range, top-end and deluxe hotels, you should have no problems organising a babysitter or finding somewhere for the kids to play. Budget hotels can be difficult if you have very little ones because the rooms are often small and noisy, and the facilities are limited and cramped. Most places will let kids under 12 stay in your room for free.

About Bangkok

HISTORY
The New Ayuthaya

Bangkok is the phoenix-risen of the Thai kingdom, the second chance after the nation's thriving capital, Ayuthaya, was devastated by Burmese invaders in 1767. In the ensuing collapse, General Taksin emerged as the primary leader, forcing out the Burmese and establishing a new capital in Thonburi, on the western bank of Mae Nam Chao Phraya (Chao Phraya River). Taksin's reunification of the country was decisive, but his ruling style was ruthless. By 1782, Chao Phraya Chakri, a key general, deposed Taksin as king and moved the capital across the river to modern-day Bangkok. Chakri's son inherited the throne, thus establishing the Chakri dynasty, which is still in place today.

Rama I (Chao Phraya Chakri) chose the eastern bank of the river as a defensive measure against possible Burmese invasions. Canals (or *khlong*) were dug to replicate the island-city of Ayuthaya and artisans were commissioned to build great temples to replace those destroyed in the old capital. The waterways were a key element in the cycle of life.

> **Tongue-Twisting Title**
> At 26 words long, Bangkok's Thai name is a bit of a mouthful, so everyone shortens it to 'Krung Thep', or 'City of Angels'. The full-length version can be translated as: 'Great city of angels, the repository of divine gems, the great land unconquerable, the grand and prominent realm, the royal and delightful capital full of nine noble gems, the highest royal dwelling and grand palace, the divine shelter and living place of reincarnated spirits'.
>
> Foreigners, however, never bothered to learn either and continued to call the capital 'Bang Makok' (Village of Olive Plums), which was eventually truncated to 'Bangkok'.

Modernisation

Reforms during the mid-18th and early 19th centuries – enacted by Rama IV (King Mongkut; 1851-68) and his son, Rama V (King Chulalongkorn;

Pure class: plentiful royal portraits mean you can't miss the royal family's importance in Thailand

Feroci & the Demo *by Joe Cummings*

In 1939, Thai Prime Minister Phibul Songkhram decided that Bangkok needed a national monument commemorating the 1932 revolution that overthrew Thailand's system of absolute monarchy. Phibul chose Th Ratchadamnoen – originally built for royal motorcades – as the ideal spot for this 'Democracy Monument' (p35). Whether he chose it specifically to thumb his nose at royalty, or because it happened to be the city's broadest avenue, is a question it's best not to ask in Thailand.

Phibul, an ardent admirer of the steely nationalism of Adolf Hitler and Benito Mussolini, chose to commission Corrado Feroci, an !talian artist who had previously designed monuments for Mussolini. Feroci in turn enlisted the help of his Thai students at Bangkok's School of Fine Arts (SOFA). Together they created a monument of structural simplicity and symbolic complexity.

To start with, Feroci and the students buried 75 cannonballs in the monument's base to signify the year of the coup, Buddhist Era 2475 (AD 1932). Atop the base they raised four Art Deco 'wings' to represent the role of the Thai army, navy, air force and police in the 1932 coup. Each wing stands 24m high, in homage to the date – 24 June – of the coup. The wings surround a turret containing a bronze cast of the original constitution, which has long been supplanted by others.

Four bas-relief human forms around the base of the wings represent the original coup conspirators, the Thai armed forces, the Thai people and the personification of 'Balance and Good Life'. Nowhere on the monument will you find any symbols of Buddhism or the monarchy.

Sculptures of the coup's conspirators are revolting even now at the Democracy Monument

1868-1910) – took the country into the modern era. Changes included the creation of a civil service, still one of Bangkok's biggest employers, eradication of slavery and successful defence of Thailand's independence during European colonisation.

You'd never know it today, but Bangkok's first road (Th Charoen Krung, also known as the 'New Road') wasn't built until the 1860s. As motorised transport took off, Bangkok expanded in every direction, often building over former canals.

The political landscape changed rapidly, too, with a bloodless coup in 1932 abruptly ending the era of absolute monarchy and ushering in a constitutional monarchy. Then in 1939 the country's official name changed from Siam to Thailand. Bangkok's infamous sex industry expanded during the Vietnam War, when it was a popular R&R stop for foreign troops.

> **Jazzin' at the Palace**
> You're more likely to hear Rama IX than see him. A jazz composer and saxophonist, he jammed with Woody Herman and Benny Goodman in his younger days and his big-band-style numbers are often played on Thai radio.

Political Upheaval & Economic Explosions

In the 1970s, democracy was on a shaky path – the military brutally suppressed a pro-democracy student rally in Bangkok and the country later see-sawed between civilian and military rule. Big demonstrations in 1992, calling for the resignation of the latest military dictator, saw violent street confrontations near Democracy Monument, resulting in 50 civilian deaths. After a right royal scolding from the king, the dictator resigned. Since 1992, the country has been ruled by democratically elected civilian coalitions.

In the last decades of the 20th century, Bangkok was the beating heart of one of Asia's hottest economies. Modern skyscrapers tickled the skyline, and the middle and upper classes developed a taste for Western luxury goods. But in 1997, the bubble burst and the Thai currency spiralled ever downwards.

Bangkok Today

The Thai economy is back on track showing more sustainable growth than in the boom-and-bust years. The new millennium ushered in two new forms of mass transit (the BTS Skytrain and MRTA Metro Subway), novelties to the traffic-choked city. Campaigns to 'clean up the city' – be it crackdowns on police corruption or early closing times for bars – have been spearheaded by Thaksin Shinawatra, Thailand's prime minister. The national government seems to desire a Singaporean ideal of conservatism and order, antithetical to Bangkok's practised chaos and tolerance. Despite the current trends, Bangkok is considered one of the most open societies in Southeast Asia.

ENVIRONMENT

Your lungs, ears and nose will tell you that Bangkok doesn't have the healthiest of environments. The air quality becomes most stultifying at major intersections, with asphyxiating vehicle emissions and particulate matter. Bangkok's also a damned noisy place round the clock, as you'll discover if you stay near a construction site jumping with jackhammers.

There has been an effort to clean up the waterways over recent decades. The results are most noticeable in the river, still used daily by residents for bathing, laundry and drinking water (after treatment). The canals on the Bangkok side are particularly murky – locals cover their faces with handkerchiefs when zipping down them by boat.

GOVERNMENT & POLITICS

Bangkok is the seat of the national government, based on the British system of constitutional monarchy. The 1997 passage of a new national constitution, ensuring more human and civil rights, has an incongruous dance partner – prime minister Thaksin Shinawatra, a telecommunications billionaire, and his Thai Rak Thai (Thais Love Thais) Party, which swept into power in January 2001 on a populist platform, garnering support from the rural provinces.

The 2004 win by Democrat governor Apirak Kosayodhin was widely regarded as a protest vote by the citizens of the capital against the authoritarian style of the prime minister, who has little tolerance for public criticism and conducts advertising-style improvement campaigns (his 'War on Drugs' is criticised as police-sanctioned vendetta killings). Despite a recent scandal over avian influenza, Thaksin remains confidently at the helm for the foreseeable future.

ECONOMY

Bangkok is Thailand's primary commercial centre: banking, finance, energy, media – you name it, the jobs are here, attracting rural villagers saddled with debt and globetrotting expats piecing together foreign correspondence work or managing operations for a multinational.

During the boom days, every man and his dog seemed to have a property investment on the boil. Half-finished and sadly abandoned apartment blocks are a constant reminder of the 1997 economic meltdown. But the country was able to take an 'early exit' from the IMF's US$17.2 billion rescue package of short-term loans in 2000. There is still lingering resentment toward the IMF and a growing antiglobalisation movement within bohemian circles.

> **DID YOU KNOW?**
> - Only 10% of Thailand's population, but 60% of its wealth, is based in Bangkok.
> - Bangkok's minimum daily wage is 162B (US$4).
> - A 1999 census found that Bangkok had 115,084 stray dogs.
> - Rama IX is the world's longest-reigning monarch.

SOCIETY & CULTURE

Although Bangkok has a distinct veneer of 'westernisation', a Thai value system is ticking away, guiding every aspect of life. When a local laughs when you trip over spectacularly, they're trying to save face on your behalf, not indulge in *Schadenfreude*. Westerners used to rapid-fire service may get frustrated with servers' lackadaisical tempo – this is just *sànùk* (fun) in action, making everything, even the most menial task, enjoyable.

When Thais get charged less to enter the museum than you, it's not because they don't like foreigners – they just think you are of higher status financially, so you should look after Thais by paying more. Status –

Orange is obviously in this year

whether it be financial, age-related or your level of power – governs every relationship.

Almost all Thais are Theravada Buddhists, aiming to be reborn into a better life by making merit (giving donations to temples or feeding monks). Every Thai male is expected to become a monk for a short time.

Etiquette

Just remember to respect two things: religion and the monarchy. This means standing when the national anthem is played (before movies and at 8am and 6pm daily); not criticising the king or his family; and dressing respectfully at royal buildings and temples (with shoulders and legs covered, and shoes removed before entering). Keep your feet pointed away from a Buddha image. Monks aren't supposed to touch or be touched by women.

When to Wâi

The traditional Thai greeting is the *wâi,* a gesture where palms are put together, prayer-like. The amount of bowing that accompanies a *wâi* is a delicate formula, dependent on the status of the two people *wâi*-ing each other. But you're best to take the attitude: if someone is *wâi*-ing you, *wâi* them back, unless they're a child or someone serving you, like a waiter.

Other ways to avoid offending Thais include: not wearing shoes inside people's homes; dressing modestly, not like you're on the beach; not touching anyone's head; not pointing your feet at people, nor touching them with your foot; and certainly not passing things to people with your left hand.

Remember to keep your cool – getting angry or talking loudly is thought rude – speak softly and smile a lot. Losing your temper is considered a major loss of face for both parties.

ARTS
Architecture

Traditional Bangkok houses were built over the river or canals on stilts, either single-room houses or houses interconnected by walkways, but always built in teak. Rooflines were steep and often decorated with spiritual motifs.

Traditional Thai architecture in Sukhumvit

The country's early artistic energies were channelled into temple (wat) architecture. Of the core components of a temple complex, the *chedi* (or stupa, where holy relics are stored) is a poignant example intersecting influences in early Thai history. A bell-shaped *chedi* is often credited to the style of Ceylon (Sri Lanka), which participated with Thailand in many monastic exchanges, and the corn-cob-shaped *praang* is an inheritance from the Khmer empire.

Ratanakosin, or old Bangkok, style (beginning in the 19th century), is a melange of Thai and European influences, exemplified by Vimanmek Teak Mansion (p16). The city started growing skyward in the 1970s.

Music

The rhythmic clinking of cymbals, the whine of the stringed *saw,* or the playful rain sounds of the *ránâat èk* (wooden xylophone) – along with the other five to 20 instruments forming a classical Thai orchestra (*pìiphâat*) – often waft over temple gates or measure ornate dance-dramas.

Keep the beat: musician playing a drum at Erawan Shrine (p27), Khannayao

---

Ear Candy
Need to know who's who in Bangkok's musical sound and fury? These are a few resounding artists and albums to know:
- *Lust For Live* (Bakery Music) Compilation featuring Modern Dog, Chou Chou, Yokee, Playboy and others from the indie label Bakery Music
- *Made in Thailand* (Carabao) The classic and international Carabao album, thanks to the eponymous song's English chorus
- *Khon Kap Khwai* (Caravan) The anthem of *phleng phêua chii-wít Best* (Pumpuang Duanjan) A collection of songs from *lûuk thûng*'s diva

---

The snake-charmer sounds of the *pìi* (oboe-like woodwind) usually accompanies Thai-boxing matches.

Modern Thai music ranges from sappy pop tunes and heartbreaking ballads to protest songs. Taxi drivers love *lûuk thûng* (literally 'children of the fields'), from the rural northeastern provinces. It has a definite croon feel to it, though the subject matter mines faithful country-and-western themes of losing your job, your wife and your buffalo. The rock bands Carabao and Caravan earned legendary status for their politically charged songs, termed *phleng phêua chii-wít* (songs for life).

Today the alternative hordes are celebrating the amorphic genre of indie, including everything from alt-rock, rap Thai and ska-funk recorded on independent labels. Tune into the radio station 104.5 FM Fat Radio or catch weekend shows at **Centrepoint Plaza** (4, D2; Siam Square Sois 3 & 4).

Theatre & Dance
Of the six traditional dramatic forms, you're most likely to come into contact with *khon*. It's extravagant and a visual feast, where hundreds

It's in the eyes: traditional dancers at Erawan Shrine (p27), Khannayao

of characters love and die, fight and dance. Acted only by men, *khon* drama is based upon stories of the *Ramayana* and was traditionally only for royal audiences.

The less formal *lákhon* dances, of which there are many dying sub-genres, usually involve costumed dancers (of both sexes) performing elements of the *Ramayana* and traditional folk tales. The most widespread variation is called *lákhon kâe bon,* which is commissioned by worshippers at shrines to earn merit.

Royal marionettes *(lákhon lék),* once on the brink of extinction, have been revived by Joe Louis Theatre (p91). The metre-high creations are elaborately costumed and perform all the subtle manipulations required of their human *khon* counterparts.

Visual Arts

Thailand's unique interpretations of Buddha images have earned the country a well-respected niche in the world of religious art. Traditional Thai painting was limited to intricate representations of *Ramakian*, Thailand's version of India's epic *Ramayana*, and *jataka,* tales of the Buddha's past lives, painted as sermons on temple walls.

Italian artist Corrado Feroci is often credited for jump-starting Thailand's secular art movement. He designed the Democracy Monument and developed the first fine arts department, now at Silpakorn University. Bangkok continues to foster Thailand's avant-garde. Internationally known Montien Boonma uses abstract symbolism to revisit traditional Buddhist themes. Reactionary artists, such as Manit Sirwanichpoom, often mix pop aesthetics with social commentary. Thaweesak Srithongdee's cheeky superheroes and sculptor Manop Suwanpinta's human anatomy pieces are confoundingly meaningless yet profound.

Jataka (stories of the Buddha's past lives) mural on the wall of Wat Suthat (p29), Phra Nakhon

Directory

Painting inside the main chapel of Wat Benchamabophit (p28), Dusit

ARRIVAL & DEPARTURE

Bangkok is a major travel hub for the region, and with the upcoming completion of the Suvanabhumi airport, capacity will increase. No frills, low cost airlines have also sprouted for short hops within Thailand and the region. Bus and train services from outside the country are more time-consuming.

Air

The new Suvanabhumi airport, in Nong Ngu Hao (Cobra Swamp), was scheduled to open in the fall of 2005 and receive all international passengers. Everyone but the prime minister anticipates that it will open around 2006 or later. For the most current information, visit the official website (www.bangkokair port.org) or the online news-sleuth at www.2Bangkok.com.

SUVANABHUMI INTERNATIONAL AIRPORT (1, C2)

Located 25km east of the city, Suvanabhumi (pronounced soo-vana-poom) airport promises to be the largest airport in Southeast Asia and able to handle Airbus A380s (555-seaters).

Information

General Inquiries ☎ 0 2723 0000

🖳 www.bangkokairport.org

Airport Access

The airport is accessible by five highway links, and estimated transit time to central Bangkok is 35 to 45 minutes.

Slotted for completion in 2006-2007, the Airport Train Link will provide express service from the airport to central Bangkok at Phayathai (cnr Th Phayathai & Phra Ram VI, with access to the Phayathai Skytrain station). According to initial planning, the express service will run every 15 minutes, take about 15 minutes to reach the airport and cost 150B to 200B. The line will also be used for commuter service – which will run every 30 minutes and take about 30 minutes, with the fare based on distance. The commuter trains will stop at eight stations between the airport and the central terminus; these include Ratchaprarop (Th Ratchaprarop near Th Sri Ayuthaya), Makkasan (near Th Phetchaburi & Th Ratchadaphisek with access to Phetchaburi subway station), and other suburban stops.

BANGKOK INTERNATIONAL AIRPORT (2, C2; DON MUANG)

Until the new airport opens, Bangkok International Airport (also known as Don Muang), 25km north of Bangkok, receives all international and domestic air traffic. Don Muang's fate is uncertain after the completion of the new airport – some sources say that it will be used for budget carriers and domestic flights, while others say that it will be retired from commercial service and transferred to the Air Force.

Transit packages are available for four-hour sightseeing tours; contact **TAT** (www.tat.or.th). Terminal 1 and 2 have left-luggage facilities. All the services (money-changers, ground transport) are available for late-night arrivals.

Information

General Inquiries ☎ 0 2535 1111

🖳 www.airportthai.co.th

Flight Information

International flights: ☎ 0 2535 1254, 0 2535 1386 (departures)

☎ 0 2535 1301, 0 2535 1149 (arrivals)

Domestic flights: ☎ 0 2535 1192 (departures)

☎ 0 2535 1253 (arrivals)

Hotel Booking Service

Thai Hotels Association booths in the arrivals halls can book accommodation for you, a process which can sometimes be complicated by the commissions they receive from hotels.

Airport Access

Trains From Don Muang station, accessible via an elevated walkway from the international terminal, trains travel to Bangkok's Hualamphong station (3, F7). Regular trains run to Bangkok from around 5am to 8pm, roughly every 45mins and cost 5B on the regular and commuter trains, and between 45B and 65B on the rapid or express trains. This trip takes around 45mins and, thanks to the new subway station at Hualamphong, final destinations in Silom and Sukhumvit are easier to reach.

Bus Depending on your hotel location, your best transport option to or from the airport may be the Airport Express (100B), which runs every half-hour from 6am to midnight. The A-1 express runs from the Silom district, A-2 from Banglamphu, A-3 from Th Sukhumvit and A-4 from Hualamphong and Siam Square. See an unofficial description of the routes and hotels served at www.bangkokbob.net/airport_bus.htm.

Taxi For late-night arrivals, a taxi is usually the path of least resistance. Ignore the taxi touts at the airport and instead head for the metered taxi desk that is located just outside the terminal. A taxi trip from the airport into the middle of Bangkok should cost you around 200B to 300B, plus tolls (40-80B) and a 50B airport fee. Don't be shy in telling the driver to put the meter on.

Bus

Government and private buses do trips from Bangkok to cities around Thailand, as well as to Malaysia. For long-distance trips, buses departing from the government bus terminals are more reliable and safer than buses leaving from tourist centres (like Th Khao San).

Three Bangkok bus terminals are for long-distance trips: Mo Chit (2, B3) serves northern and northeastern Thailand and is accessible by Skytrain (Mo Chit station) and then transfer to bus No 8. Ekamai (2, C5) serves eastern cities (Pattaya and Ko Samet) and is accessible via Ekamai Skytrain station. Sai Tai Mai (2, A4) is in Thonburi and serves the south; take bus No 30.

Train

From Hualamphong (3, F7), the main train station, there are five rail spurs – north to Chiang Mai, northeast to Nong Khai and Ubon Ratchathani (two lines that split at Khorat), southeast to Aranya Prathet (a border crossing-point to Cambodia) and south to Malaysia. Hualamphong has left-luggage facilities, although it is probably wiser to arrange this service at your hotel. In Thonburi, Bangkok Noi (3, A3) train station handles short-line routes to Kanchanaburi; there are no left-luggage facilities here.

To reserve seats call ☎ 0 2220 4444 or visit the advance booking office at Hualamphong. Trains come in three classes – from cattle car to comfy fold-out beds. The website www.seat61.com has helpful train-planning advice.

Travel Documents
PASSPORT

To enter Thailand, your passport must be valid for six months from the date of entry.

VISAS

Residents of Australia, Canada, New Zealand, South Africa, the UK and the USA can stay in Bangkok for 30 days without a visa. If you plan on a longer trip, apply for a 60-day tourist visa or a 90-day non-immigrant visa before you leave home. You can also apply for a visa extension from the **Immigration Office** (4, F6; ☎ 02 287 3101 10, Soi Suan Phlu, Th Sathon Tai); see the **Ministry of Foreign Affairs website** (www.mfa.go.th) for more information. Neighbouring countries also maintain embassies in Bangkok from which you can apply for a visa, but allow plenty of time.

Do all visa applications and extensions in person rather than relying on a service to do it for you. Several travellers have been arrested prior to their air departure from Thailand because of forged visa stamps acquired through agents.

RETURN/ONWARD TICKET

Technically, you're supposed to demonstrate proof of a return or onward ticket; however, in practice, you are unlikely to be asked to show it.

Customs

You are not permitted to bring illegal drugs, firearms or pornography into Thailand.

Duty Free

Visitors can bring in 1L of wine or spirits, 200 cigarettes or 250g of other smoking material without paying duty.

Departure Tax

International travellers have to pay a separate 500B departure tax after checking in at the airline counter, while domestic travellers pay a 30B departure tax in the price of their ticket.

GETTING AROUND

It can be tricky to decipher and pronounce Thailand's addresses. *'Thanon'* is a street, a *'soi'* is a laneway that runs off a bigger street and a *'trok'* is an alley. In this book, 'Soi 6, Th Sukhumvit' means that Soi 6 runs off Th Sukhumvit. Building numbers often have confusing slashes and dashes, like 325/7-8 Th Charoen Krung. This stems from an old system of allocating property; the prefix in the address will be a helpful locator once you arrive on the street, but don't count on it as an indicator of the building's proximity to an intersection.

Bus

Buses are very useful in Banglamphu and Chinatown (which aren't served by trains). Non-aircon buses (red, green and white-and-blue) cost 3.5B to 5B. Air-con buses (blue) charge between 8B and 18B; Euro buses (orange) charge 10B for the first kilometre, plus 2B for each additional kilometre.

The Tour 'n' Guide Map *Bangkok Thailand* shows routes but has not been updated to indicated the prefix addition of '50' to most air-conditioned routes. Hold on to your ticket as proof of purchase (an occasional formality).

Skytrain

The Skytrain has revolutionised travel around the newer districts of Bangkok. Trains arrive every few minutes from 6am to midnight. Tickets cost from 10B to 40B. Skytrain's three-day tourist pass (280B) with unlimited trips is good for more than 10 trips; otherwise opt for the 250/160B (including 30B refundable deposit) 10-ride pass.

Free shuttle buses on particular routes can drop you at Skytrain stations – check out www.bts.co.th for routes – and run from 6.30am to 10.30pm.

Subway

The first line of Bangkok's subway opened in 2004 and connects the railway station of Bang Sue with Chatuchak (Mo Chit Skytrain station), Thailand Culture Centre, Sukhumvit (with access to Asoke Skytrain station), Queen Sirikit Convention Centre, Lumphini Park, Silom (with access to Sala Daeng Skytrain station) and terminating at Hualamphong. Trains operate from 5am to midnight and cost 14B to 36B, depending on distance. Future extensions will connect Hualamphong to Chinatown and Thonburi.

For short-term visitors, the subway makes Hualamphong and the convention centre easier to reach from Silom and Sukhumvit.

Boat

For sights in Banglamphu, Ko Ratanakosin and some parts of Silom, the **Chao Phraya Express Boat** (☎ 0 2617 7340; www.chao phrayaboat.com) is the most convenient option. The service runs from 6am to 7.30pm; you can buy tickets (6B to 25B) on board. Boats with yellow or red-and-orange flags are expresses, running during peak times, and so don't make every stop. A **tourist boat** (15B; ⏲ 9.30am-4pm) runs from Tha Sathon (with access to Saphan Taksin Skytrain station) with stops at 10 major sight-seeing piers; a 75B unlimited day-pass is also available. Hold on to your ticket as proof of purchase (an occasional formality).

Longtail **khlong taxis** zip around the Bangkok's Khlong Saen Saeb, conducting quick but sometimes smelly trips from Tha Withayu (4, G1), Tha Pratunam (4, F1) and Tha Ratchathewi (4, D1) to Tha Phan Fah (4, D4; near Wat Saket). Fares cost from 5B to 8B and the service runs from 6am to 7pm.

At all boat piers, private longtail boats can be hired for sightseeing trips (p52).

Taxi

Taxis in Bangkok are plentiful but victims of traffic vagaries. Always take the meter taxis and insist on using the meters. Don't take taxis that quote a price, which is typically three times higher than the metered price. You pay a 35B flag fall, then 4.5B/km for trips between 2km and 12km, 5B/km between 13km and 20km and 5.5B/km for more than 20km; in a traffic jam you pay 1.25B a minute. You pay a 50B surcharge for trips leaving the airport and all tolls. Report complaints to ☎ 0 2272 5460.

Túk-Túk

These putt-putting three-wheeled vehicles are tourist-traps that will zip you to an overpriced tailor or jewellery shop regardless of your intended destination. For kicks, take them for short hops (within a neighbourhood); 40B is usually a fair price. Refuse to enter any unrequested shop. Skip the 10B sight-seeing offers.

Motorcycle Taxi

Need to be somewhere in a hurry during rush hour? A jaunt on a motorcycle taxi is guaranteed to be super-quick and (hopefully) death-defying. Short journeys cost around 20B. Women wearing skirts should ride side-saddle.

Car & Motorcycle

You're either extremely patient or mad to drive in Bangkok. Even once you get somewhere, parking is usually a nightmare. You'll pay around 16B/L for petrol.

ROAD RULES

Appearances may be deceiving, but there are road rules in Bangkok. The current government is having a major crackdown on motorists breaking the rules by driving on the wrong (right-hand) side of the road and not wearing seatbelts.

RENTAL

Car hire starts at around 1500B per day, but the rate often gets cheaper if you hire by the week or month. Rental companies include **Avis** (4, G2; ☎ 0 2255 5300; 2/12 Th Withayu; ☀ 8am-6pm) and **Budget** (2, C2; ☎ 0 2552 8921; Bangkok International Airport).

DRIVING LICENCE & PERMIT

You are required to have an International Driving Permit to drive in Bangkok.

MOTORING ORGANISATIONS

If your car breaks down, you could try getting in touch with **Carworld Club** (☎ 0 2260 1111), which offers roadside assistance.

PRACTICALITIES
Climate & When to Go

The cooler and drier time to visit Bangkok is between November and February, though this time, as well as March and August, is the peak season. Between April and May it's unbearably hot, while in September and October (during the rainy season), parts of the city are prone to flooding.

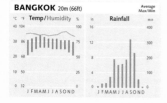

Disabled Travellers

Movement around the streets of Bangkok can be a complete nightmare for someone with impaired mobility – there are few sloping kerbs or wheelchair ramps, and many streets are best crossed via stair-heavy pedestrian crossings. Some disabled travellers hire a taxi or a private car and driver to see the sights, rather than taking tours, although it can be difficult to fit a wheelchair in the taxi boot. Five Skytrain stations have lifts: Asoke, Chong Nonsi, Mo Chit, On Nut and Siam Square. You can travel for free from these stations if you show your disabled association membership. Some hotel chains, like Amari and Banyan Tree, are particularly aware of the needs of disabled travellers.

INFORMATION & ORGANISATIONS

Gimp on the Go (www.gimponthego.com)

Society for Accessible Travel & Hospitality (www.sath.org)

Discounts

Discounts are given to students on Skytrain passes and children's fares are available at some attractions.

Electricity

Electric currents in Thailand are 220V, 50 cycles. Most electrical wall outlets take the round, two-prong terminals, but some will take flat, two-bladed terminals and others will take both. It's easier to bring a converter from home than to waste time trying to hunt down an electrical store in Bangkok.

Embassies

Australia (7, C3; ☎ 0 2287 2680; www.austembassy.or.th; 37 Th Sathon Tai)

Cambodia (4, E4; ☎ 0 2254 6630; www.cambodia.gov.kh; 185 Th Ratchadamri)

Canada (7, D2; ☎ 0 2636 0540; www.dfait-maeci.gc.ca/Bangkok; 15th fl, Abdulrahim Bldg, 990 Th Phra Ram IV)

Ireland (7, D3; ☎ 0 2638 0303; 48/20, 12th Floor, TISCO Tower, Th Sathon Neua)

Laos (2, C4; ☎ 0 2539 6667; www .bkklaoembassy.com; 520/1-3 Soi 39, Th Ramkhamhaeng)

Myanmar (Burma; 4, C6; ☎ 0 2233 2237; 132 Th Sathon Neua)

New Zealand (4, G3; ☎ 0 2254 2530; www.nzembassy.com; 14th fl, All Seasons Place Bldg, 87 Th Withayu)

UK (4, G2; ☎ 0 2305 8333; www .britishembassy.gov.uk; 1031 Th Withayu)

USA (4, G3; ☎ 0 2205 4000; bangkok .usembassy.gov; 120-22 Th Withayu)

Emergency Numbers

Ambulance	☎ 1646
Fire	☎ 199
Police	☎ 191
Tourist Police	☎ 1155

Fitness

Although it would appear that all these thin mints are just metabolically lucky, Lumphini Park (4, F4) and Sanam Luang (3, B4) betray the city's devotion to exercise. More like a disco than a gym, **California Fitness Center** (☎ 0 2631 1122; cnr Th Convent & Th Silom) is part of the 24-Hour Fitness network. **Clark Hatch Physical Fitness Centres** (www .clarkhatchthailand.com) has five branches throughout the city and all the work-out sundries.

Gay & Lesbian Travellers

As you'll soon notice, Thai culture is incredibly tolerant of homosexuality, but public displays of affection, whether you're gay or straight, are no-nos. The 'pink triangle' of Th Silom, Th Surawong and Th Sathon is an area with loads of bars, cafés and saunas. The lesbian scene is much more low-key and not centred in the entertainment districts.

INFORMATION & ORGANISATIONS

Dreaded Ned's website (www .dreadedned.com)

Long Yang Club (☎ 02 2677 6965; www.longyangclub.org)

Lesla (www.lesla.com)

Health
IMMUNISATIONS

You don't really need vaccinations, unless you are travelling outside Bangkok, but make sure your tetanus and polio boosters are up to date. You will need to show proof of vaccination if you're coming from a yellow-fever-infected area, like Africa or parts of South America.

PRECAUTIONS

It's not uncommon to get a mild case of 'Bangkok belly' as your digestive system adjusts to your new diet and environment. Don't drink the Bangkok tap water, nor use it to clean your teeth, but it's perfectly OK to drink the water served in restaurants and hotels as it has been purified. Malaria is not a problem in Bangkok but you should always try to avoid getting bitten by mosquitoes, as there are occasional reports of dengue fever in Bangkok. The mosquito that transmits the virus is most active during the day.

To ensure you can keep dehydration and heat fatigue at bay, drink lots of fluids, walk in the shade and rest during the mid-afternoon. If you do get Bangkok belly, be vigilant about fluid replacement. Like anywhere else, practise the usual precautions when it comes to sex; condoms are widely available from chemists and supermarkets.

MEDICAL SERVICES

Hospitals that have 24-hour accident and emergency departments include:

BNH Hospital (7, C3; ☎ 0 2632 0550; 9/1 Th Convent, Th Silom)

Bumrungrad Hospital (4, H2; ☎ 0 2667 1000; 33 Soi 3, Th Sukhumvit)

Samitivej Hospital (2, B5; ☎ 0 2711 8000; 133 Soi 49, Th Sukhumvit)

DENTAL SERVICES

If you chip your tooth or require emergency treatment then take yourself to the dental clinic at a major hospital like Bumrungrad (see above).

PHARMACIES

Pharmacies can be found everywhere in Bangkok, can treat the most common travellers' complaints and have English-speaking staff.

Holidays

Lunar holidays change each year; check out the **TAT website** (www .tat.or.th).

1 January	New Year's Day
January-March	Magha Puja (lunar)
6 April	Chakri Day
April	Songkhran Festival (lunar)
5 May	Coronation Day
May	Visakha Puja (lunar)
July	Asalha Puja (lunar)
July	Khao Phansa (lunar)
12 August	Queen's Birthday
23 October	Chulalongkorn Day
5 December	King's Birthday
10 December	Constitution Day

Internet & Digital Resources

Internet access is widely available at Internet cafés, starting at 0.5B per minute, and at shopping centres starting at 1B per minute. Several online directories list wireless Internet hotspots in Bangkok.

USEFUL SITES

Lonely Planet www.lonelyplanet.com
Bangkok Metro www.bkkmetro.com
Bangkok Post www.bangkokpost.net
Bangkok Thailand Today www .bangkok.thailandtoday.com
The Nation www.nationmultimedia.com
Tourism Authority of Thailand www .tat.or.th

Lost Property

For lost items on a bus call ☎ 184, on Skytrain call ☎ 0 2617 7300 and on Chao Phraya River Express boats call ☎ 0 2225 3002/3.

Metric System

Thailand uses the metric system except when measuring land, which is often quoted using the traditional system of *waa, ngaan and râi*. See also the conversion table.

TEMPERATURE
°C = (°F - 32) ÷ 1.8
°F = (°C x 1.8) + 32

DISTANCE
1in = 2.54cm
1cm = 0.39in
1m = 3.3ft = 1.1yd
1ft = 0.3m
1km = 0.62 miles
1 mile = 1.6km

WEIGHT
1kg = 2.2lb
1lb = 0.45kg
1g = 0.04oz
1oz = 28g

VOLUME
1L = 0.26 US gallons
1 US gallon = 3.8L
1L = 0.22 imperial gallons
1 imperial gallon = 4.55L

Money

CURRENCY

The basic unit of Thai currency is the baht (B), made up of 100 satang. Notes come in denominations of 20B, 50B, 100B, 500B and 1000B, while coins come in 1B, 5B and 10B and occasionally 25 satang or 50 satang. Go to 7-Eleven shops or other reputable places to break 1000B notes; don't expect a vendor or taxi to have change for a note 500B or larger.

TRAVELLERS CHEQUES

Travellers cheques are easily cashed for a commission at major banks in Bangkok. Buy cheques in US dollars or British pounds to avoid possible hassles.

CREDIT CARDS

You'll have few problems using your credit card – especially if it's a Visa, MasterCard, Diners Club or AmEx – at most higher-end hotels and restaurants. For 24-hr card cancellations or assistance, call:

American Express (☎ 0 2273 5544)
Diners Club (☎ 0 2238 3660)
MasterCard (☎ 0 2260 8572)
Visa (☎ 0 2256 7326)

ATMS

Automatic Teller Machines are widespread and usually accept Cirrus, Plus, Maestro, JCB and Visa cards.

CHANGING MONEY

The banks offer the best rates for changing money. They're generally open from 10am to 4pm Monday to Friday but some have currency exchange counters that operate from 8am to 8pm.

TIPPING

Tipping practices vary in Thailand, but many mid-range and expensive restaurants add a 10% service charge to the bill in addition to a 7% VAT (value-added tax).

Newspapers & Magazines

Bangkok has two English-language broadsheets: *Bangkok Post* and The *Nation*. See the Shopping chapter for recommendations on newsstands and bookstores.

Opening Hours

Bangkok is predominantly an on-the-go-seven-days-a-week town. Restaurants generally open from around 10am to 10pm, shops from 10am to 8pm. Businesses along Th Charoen Krung close on Sunday.

Photography & Video

Print and slide film and VHS video cassettes are widely available and inexpensive. There are many film-processing labs, with good rates, throughout the city. Thailand uses the PAL video system, which is compatible with Europe (except France) and Australia. Some video shops sell NTSC format tapes, compatible with the USA and Japan.

Post

Thailand has an efficient national postal service. The main post office (3, F9) is on Th Charoen Krung, between Sois 32 and 34. Another post office (6, C2) is on Th Tani in Banglamphu, near Th Khao San; both offer telecommunications. Handy postal codes include:

Bangrak	10500
Khlong Toey	10110
Pathumwan	10330
Ratchadamnoen	10200

Don't send any valuables or cash through the post and don't lick any stamps as most bear a picture of the King.

POSTAL RATES

You'll pay between 12B and 15B to send a postcard anywhere in the world. Letter-writers will pay 17B to post to Australasia and Europe, and 19B to the Americas.

OPENING HOURS

The GPO is open from 8am to 8pm Monday to Saturday and 8am to 1pm Sunday and holidays, while post office agencies operate from 8.30am to 5.30pm Monday to Friday and 9am to noon Saturday.

Radio

Bangkok has over 70 radio stations, many of them broadcasting in Thai and English. FMX (95.5FM) and Get Radio (102.5FM) have bilingual DJs playing rock, R&B and pop.

Safety Concerns

You are more likely to be conned in Bangkok than attacked. Be wary of friendly strangers offering cigarettes, food and drink, as some people have been known to mix heavy sedatives in them – men have often been victims. Beware of the ubiquitous gem scam, lock all valuables in the hotel safe and don't trust unsolicited endorsements of tailors or jewellery shops.

Senior Travellers

You'll be shown great respect in this elder-worshipping culture. Most older Thais dye their hair, so you might get looks for your well-earned crown of grey or white. Bangkok can be a difficult place to get around, with plenty of broken footpaths, stairs and crazy drivers to contend with. Seniors' discounts or organisations are minimal too.

Telephone

Phone booths are widespread and well-marked as being local or international, phone card- or change-accepting.

PHONE CARDS

Phone cards are widely available and will cost you 100B for domestic and 300B for international cards.

MOBILE PHONES

Arrange global roaming for your mobile phone before you get to Bangkok.

COUNTRY & CITY CODES

All Thai phone numbers now have eight digits.

Thailand	☎ 66
Bangkok	☎ 02

Useful Numbers

Local Directory Inquiries	☎ 1133
International Directory	☎ 100
International Operator	☎ 100
Reverse-Charge (collect)	☎ 100

International Direct Dial Codes

Dial ☎ 001 followed by:

Australia	☎ 61
Canada	☎ 1
Japan	☎ 81
New Zealand	☎ 64
South Africa	☎ 27
UK	☎ 44
USA	☎ 1

Television

Of the five TV stations, two (channels 5 and 7) are owned by the military, two (channels 9 and 11) by the government and one (channel 3) is in private hands. Cable TV in Thailand is run by UBC, which has MTV Asia, BBC World and CNN.

Time

Bangkok Standard Time is seven hours ahead of GMT/UTC. At noon in Bangkok it's:

midnight in New York
9pm the previous day in Los Angeles
5am in London
7am in Johannesburg
3pm in Sydney
5pm in Auckland

Toilets

Public toilets can be found in department stores, hotels and tourist sites. Though most toilets you'll see will be of the Western sit-down variety, you may come across squat toilets. Next to these toilets is a bucket of water with a plastic bowl; use the water to wash yourself on the toilet and then later flush waste into the septic system. Never flush paper down these toilets. Often sit-down toilets have a bucket of used toilet paper next to them – a sign that you should do the same.

Tourist Information
TOURIST INFORMATION ABROAD

Australia & New Zealand (☎ 02-9247 7549; 2nd fl, 75 Pitt St, Sydney, NSW 2000)
UK (☎ 07 925 2511; 3rd fl, Brook House, 98-99 Jermyn St, London \ SW1Y 6EE)
USA & Canada (☎ 323-461-9814; 611 N Larchmont Blvd, 1st fl, Los Angeles, CA 90004)

LOCAL TOURIST INFORMATION

Beware of bogus tourist offices or officials purporting to be the real deal.
Bangkok Tourist Bureau (6, A2; ☎ 0 2225 7612-5; 17/1 Th Phra Athit; ☺ 9am-7pm) yellow information booths throughout the city
Tourist Authority of Thailand (2, B4; TAT; ☎ 0 2250 5500; 1600 Th Phet chaburi Tat Mai; ☺ 8.30am-4.30pm)

TAT airport information desk (2, C1; arrival hall, Terminal 1 & 2, Bangkok International Airport; ☺ 8am-midnight)
Tourist Police (3, D3; ☎ 1155; Th Ratchadamnoen Nok) for reporting crimes

Travel Insurance

A policy covering theft, loss, medical expenses and compensation for cancellation or delays in your travel arrangements is highly recommended. If items are lost or stolen, make sure you get a police report or your insurer might not pay up.

Women Travellers

Women would be wise not to travel alone at night, especially in *túk-túk*, and should stay at a hotel or guesthouse with good security and ensure their rooms are secure. Tampons and the contraceptive pill are easily available from chemists, though the range of brands is not extensive.

LANGUAGE

Thailand's official language is Thai. The dialect from Central Thailand has been adopted as the lingua franca, though regional dialects are still spoken. Thai is a tonal language, with five tones. Written Thai is read from left to right. Transliteration of Thai into the Roman alphabet renders multiple (and contradictory) spellings. After every sentence, men affix the polite particle *'kháp'*, and women *'khá'*.

BASICS

Greetings/Hello.	sàwàt-dii
Goodbye.	laa kàwn
How are you?	sàbai dii mǎi?
I'm fine.	sàbai dii
Please.	kà-rú-naa

Thank you.	khàwp khun	1	nèung
Excuse me.	khǎw thôht	2	sǎwng
What's your	khun chêu à-	3	sǎam
name?	rai?	4	sìi
My name is…		5	hâa
(men)	phǒm chêu…	6	hòk
(women)	dì-chǎn	7	jèt
	chêu…	8	pàet
		9	kâo
		10	sìp
I understand.	khâo jai	11	sìp-èt
I don't	mâi khâo	12	sìp-sǎwng
understand.	jai	13	sìp-sǎam
How much?	thâo-rai?	20	yîi-sìp
Help!	chûay dûay!	21	yîi-sìp-èt
Stop!	yùt!	22	yîi-sìp-sǎwng
		30	sǎam-sìp
TIME & NUMBERS		40	sìi-sìp
What's the	kìi mohng	50	hâa-sìp
time?	láew?	100	ráwy
today	wan níi	200	sǎwng ráwy
tomorrow	phrûng níi	1000	phan
yesterday	mêu·a waan	one million	láan

Index

See also separate indexes for Eating (p126), Sleeping (p126), Shopping (p126) and Sights (p127; including map references).

EATING

SLEEPING

SHOPPING

Sights Index

FEATURES

[Chennai Kitchen] .... *Eating*
[National Theatre] .... *Entertainment*
[The Barbican] .... *Drinking*
[Coffee Society] .... *Café*
[Golden Mount] .... *Highlights*
[Jim Thompson] .... *Shopping*
[National Gallery] ..... *Sights/Activities*
[Banyan Tree] .... *Sleeping*

AREAS

.... Beach, Desert
.... Building
.... Land
.... Mall
.... Other Area
.... Park/Cemetary
.... Sports
.... Urban

HYDROGRAPHY

.... River, Creek
.... Intermittent River
.... Canal
.... Swamp
.... Water

BOUNDARIES

.... State, Provincial
.... Regional, Suburb
.... Ancient Wall

ROUTES

.... Tollway
.... Freeway
.... Primary Road
.... Secondary Road
.... Tertiary Road
.... Lane
.... Under Construction
.... One-Way Street
.... Unsealed Road
.... Mall/Steps
.... Tunnel
.... Walking Path
.... Walking Trail
.... Track
.... Walking Tour

TRANSPORT

.... Airport, Airfield
.... Bus Route
.... Cycling, Bicycle Path
.... Ferry
.... General Transport
.... Subway
.... Skytrain
.... Rail
.... Taxi Rank
.... Tram

SYMBOLS

.... Bank, ATM
.... Buddhist
.... Castle, Fortress
.... Christian
.... Embassy, Consulate
.... Hindu
.... Hospital, Clinic
.... Information
.... Internet Access
.... Islamic
.... Jewish
.... Lighthouse
.... Lookout
.... Monument
.... Mountain, Volcano
.... National Park
.... Parking Area
.... Petrol Station
.... Point of Interest
.... Police Station
.... Post Office
.... Ruin
.... Sikh
.... Telephone
.... Toilets
.... Zoo, Bird Sanctuary
.... Waterfall

24/7 travel advice
www.lonelyplanet.com